forever

Simple Things Matter in Love and Marriage

2^{00}

Twenty-six years of research on successful

love and marriage has taught us many things,

but first and foremost –

no love has blossomed or been sustained

without doing the "simple things."

Simple Things Matter

in Love and Marriage

By the Authors of
Golden Anniversaries: The Seven Secrets of Successful Marriage

2009 Mom's Choice Awards Winner - Most Outstanding Relationships and Marriage Book

2009 Nautilus Book Awards Winner - Relationships

2008 INDIE Book Awards Winner - Best Relationship Book

Dr. Charles D. Schmitz

Dean and Professor of Counseling and Family Therapy
University of Missouri-St. Louis

Dr. Elizabeth A. Schmitz

President, Successful Marriage Reflections, LLC

"America's #1 Love and Marriage Experts"

Published by Briarcliff Publishing

This book is the result of over 26 years of research by the authors with successfully married couples in the United States and around the world. The stories and anecdotes in this book are based on their research and in all cases, names and identifying information have been changed except when permission was granted to reveal their actual names.

Book design by Sandy Morris and Elizabeth Schmitz

Book cover by Sandy Morris

Photographs by Pat Romano and August Jennewein

Library of Congress Cataloging-in-Publication Data.

Schmitz, Charles D., 1946-

Simple things matter : in love and marriage /

by Charles D. Schmitz, Elizabeth A. Schmitz. – 1st ed.

p. cm.

ISBN 978-0-9800554-4-3 (alk. paper)

1. Marriage. 2. Love. 3. Man-woman relationships.

I. Schmitz, Elizabeth A., 1948- II. Title.

HQ519.S365 2009

646.7'8--dc22

2009015594

Summary: Capturing the essence of over 26 years of interviews with successfully married couples in the USA and around the world, Simple Things Matter demonstrates that first and foremost – no love has blossomed or been sustained without doing the simple things. Big things don't matter until you have mastered the art of doing the simple things day in and day out in your relationship.

Printed by Walsworth Publishing Company

PRINTED IN THE UNITED STATES OF AMERICA

10 9 8 7 6 5 4 3 2 1

First Edition

WE DEDICATE THIS BOOK *to the hundreds of successfully married couples we have interviewed over these past 26 years and to our own enduring love for each other.*

About the Authors

DRS. CHARLES AND ELIZABETH SCHMITZ are renowned love and marriage experts and multiple award winning authors. As "The Official Guides To Marriage" for www.SelfGrowth.com – the number one self-help website in the world– they have established a vast worldwide readership.

The distinguished careers of Drs. Charles and Elizabeth Schmitz include more than 65 awards, 350 books, articles and manuscripts, and over 1000 speeches. As America's #1 Love and Marriage Experts, they frequently appear on radio, television, the Internet and in the print media.

With more than 26 years of research experience on relationships and successful marriage around the world, as well as their own 42-year marriage, the Doctors know what makes relationships, love and marriage work. Their recent book, ***Golden Anniversaries: The Seven Secrets of Successful Marriage***, won the 2009 Mom's Choice Awards Gold Medal for Most Outstanding Relationships and Marriage Book, the 2008 INDIE Book Awards Gold Medal for Best Relationship Book, and the 2009 Nautilus Book Award for Relationships.

Dr. Charles D. Schmitz has been a highly successful faculty member and administrator in higher education for 39 years. He received his Ph.D. from the University of Missouri – Columbia and is currently Dean of the College of Education at the University of Missouri – St. Louis and Professor of Counseling and Family Therapy.

Dr. Elizabeth A. Schmitz is president of Successful Marriage Reflections, LLC. She was an award-winning educator and administrator for 36 years. She received her doctoral degree from the University of Missouri – Columbia and has lectured in numerous college courses in the areas of counseling and leadership.

Contents

About the Research

"'TIL DEATH DO US PART" are the words couples use in committing their lives to each other. It is the promise we made to each other 42 years ago and to this day we have a lasting love that burns even brighter now than when we first said, "I do." Why has our love lasted when so many of our friends have long since ended their marriages in divorce? This is the question we began researching more than 26 years ago.

We continually remind others that the divorce rate in America is 35-40%, not the oft-reported 50%. Still, the divorce rate is too high by any measure. But the news gets worse. Close to two-thirds of those who get remarried get divorced again! And 75% of those who marry for the third time get divorced. And the simple truth is, most all of this suffering and unhappiness could be avoided. Yes, avoided! How, you say? Well, successfully married couples can tell you. They know!

That is why we have committed our lives to increasing the success rate of marriage by sharing what we have learned from decades of research and our own 42 years of marriage – ***most marriages are worth saving and can be saved!!***

We have taken a ***completely different approach in our research*** – we decided that the best way to understand how to make marriage a success is to study ***successful marriages.*** You cannot learn about success by studying failure. Success is not the absence of failure but rather the joy and beauty of happiness in a successful marriage.

Over the past 26 years, we have gathered more than ***15,000 years of collective wisdom*** from happily and successfully married couples in the USA and around the world – people of different ages, ethnicities and faiths.

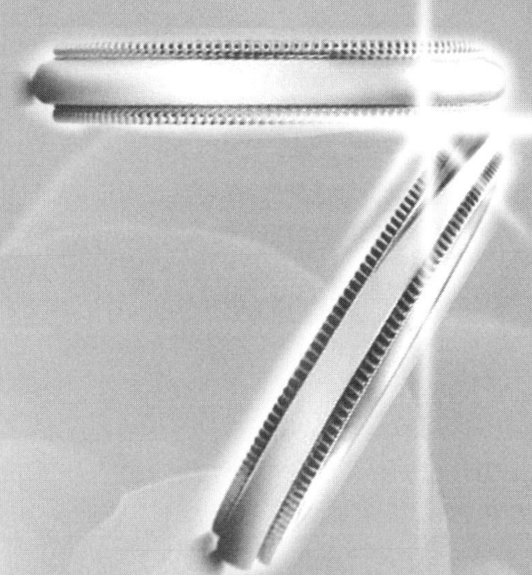

THE SEVEN QUESTIONS

We have learned in our 26 years of research on successful marriage on five continents and over forty countries of the world that there are seven questions that are most frequently asked about love and marriage. *Simple Things Matter In Love and Marriage* focuses on the answers to these seven important questions:

WHAT IS LOVE?

HOW CAN I FIND LOVE?

HOW WILL I KNOW I'M IN LOVE?

WHAT ARE THE SIMPLE THINGS THAT MATTER?

WHAT MAKES LOVE LAST?

HOW CAN MARRIAGE SURVIVE CHALLENGES?

WHY IS LOVE MORE SPECIAL ON HOLIDAYS?

Introduction

TWENTY-SIX YEARS OF RESEARCH ON successful love and marriage has taught us many things, but first and foremost – no love has blossomed or been sustained without doing the "simple things." Big things don't matter until your relationship has mastered the art of doing the simple things day in and day out in your relationship with another human being whom you purport to love.

All too often in life, people make assumptions about love and relationships that do not stand up under scrutiny – that are not supported by the available evidence. So, what are the facts?

One of the great misconceptions of all time about love and relationships is this – just do the "big" things and everything will turn out well. And what do the Big Things include? For starters the list includes "having financial stability in your relationship," "being in love is all that matters," "having a good job and a house in the suburbs," and so it goes. But the truth is, these "Big Things" are important, but they are only a by-product of "doing the simple things." Here's what we mean.

If you want your marriage and your relationship to succeed, just do the simple things! Do them day in and day out. When your relationship has mastered the "simple things" you have a chance to make it work. You have a chance to make it last. But if you don't, well, failure becomes an option.

There is another important fact of life when it comes to love and relationships – there will be big challenges to address in your relationships, of that you can be sure. You might have to deal with financial setbacks, serious illness, the loss of a job, or the death of a loved one. And trust us on this – if your relationship with the one you love has mastered the art of doing the simple things day in and day out, the likelihood of your relationship making it through the tough times are multiplied many times over.

So what are these simple things? Here are a few: always showing respect for the one you love; saying I love you many times a day; engaging in simple acts of kindness (breakfast in bed, flowers on non-special occasions; opening doors for them, etc.); giving your lover lots of daily hugs; treating them with courtesy at all times; helping clean up the dinner table; sharing financial decisions with them, and the list goes on. This book, *Simple Things Matter In Love and Marriage,* is filled with examples and tips about how to "just do" the simple things.

The point is, simple things matter and when you practice doing them, they accumulate. Simple acts add up. And always remember, you can't keep turning on then turning off doing the simple things. You have to consistently engage in doing the simple things day in and day out. When you do, you will be surprised at how well this simple notion works.

We hope our little book of essays will help you reap a bountiful harvest of love on your journey of life. Start today. Love well!

Please check www.GoldenAnniversaries.com regularly to find new books, articles, DVDs and everything you need to discover how to make love last for a lifetime.

The Perfect Wedding! Now What?

You've had a perfect wedding
and now you have a glimpse
of what can come next if only you will
commit to these simple notions.

THE BRIDE LOOKED GORGEOUS in her beautiful wedding dress, the groom looked handsome and dashing, and the marriage ceremony was a fairy tale that had come true. When she tossed her bouquet of flowers into the crowd after the wedding, a mad scramble ensued to determine who the next lucky bride would be. All was well with the world.

Weddings are so much fun! The memories of such a joyous moment will linger for a lifetime in the minds of most who witnessed it. The photos of the wedding will hang on the wall of their new home, be stored in the photo albums of many, and fill up digital space in their iPhoto collection on their computer hard-drive. For the majority of those getting married, the recall of this significant moment in their lives together will occur frequently and exist in their repertoire of positive reflections "Until death do us part."

Getting married is, however, the easy part for most couples. *Being* married is when the difficult work begins. And all too often, married couples find it difficult to get beyond the wedding in their relationship with each other. When the luster of the fairy tale starts to wear off and the difficult part of making a marriage work begins, many newly married couples flounder – they stumble – and sometimes, they fall. But you know what, this can all be prevented if you just follow the ***five simple steps*** we have learned from successfully married couples over more than 25 years of research.

First a few overarching rules of marital engagement:

Rule number one – Knowing what makes marriage work is simple to understand.

Rule number two – You have to just do the simple things required to make marriage work.

Rule number three – Successful marriage is an accumulation of doing the simple things day in and day out of your marriage.

We tell newly married couples to commit these three simple rules to memory and to practice from Day 1 if they expect their marriage to succeed. Successful marriage follows only after these important rules are learned.

Now, you are ready for the five simple steps. Here goes.

1. Commit yourselves after the Honeymoon is over to sit down together and share with each other what you want and expect from your marriage. Lay it all on the table. What are your collective and individual expectations for the marriage? How does each want to be treated by your spouse? Are there housekeeping issues that need to be addressed? What are the democratic values you bring to the marriage? Do you have plans for children and if so, when? What about your individual educational plans? Where do you want to call home now and in the foreseeable future? And the list goes on. The point is, issues like these must be addressed early in the marriage and they must be addressed directly. Questions cannot usually be answered if the questions are not asked. Issues cannot be dealt with if you don't know what the issues are. And the truth is, Step 1 is the necessary first step in building a relationship of communication, give and take, truthfulness, and trust, so necessary to building a lasting love.

2. It is important early on in a marriage to commit each other to the "core values" you want in your marriage. For example, successfully married couples are committed to the notion that they always put their spouse first in their relationship with each other. Marriage is not a "me" experience. Marriage is a "we" experience. Putting your needs before that of your partner is not a core value either of you should commit to. Rather, putting each other first lays the foundation upon which your new marriage can build. In addition, committing to caring and unconditional love for each other strengthens the foundation of your marriage. Being mutually responsible, trustworthy, and respectable towards each other adds to the fullness and richness of your relationship. Commitment to these core values will serve your marriage well over the years.

3. Recognize and accept the fact that good sex is not the heart of your marriage! This is the hardest lesson to learn after the honeymoon is over and the realities of everyday living in a marital relationship begin to take over. Sex can be a wonderful way to establish intimacy with the one you love. There is no debate about that. But on the other hand, if you set sexual expectations high on your list of things that will make your marriage fulfilling, you will quickly discover that sex alone will not make it so. Your marriage will make it for a whole bunch of reasons, but healthy sex is only one of them. In our book, *Golden Anniversaries: The Seven Secrets of Successful Marriage*, we report many first hand accounts from successfully married couples who report how important intimacy is to a loving marriage. They hug each other often, they kiss, they touch each other while talking, they sit cheek to cheek on the couch while having a conversation, they curl around each other when they sleep or just gaze at the stars, and yes, they have sex from time to time – when it's right for them. Keep sexual intimacy in perspective in your marriage. Commit to that notion from Day 1.

4. Remember this important rule – actions speak louder than words! Early in your marriage you must commit to the simple truth that you will be judged by your actions and deeds, not by your words. When you commit to something with your words, your actions must follow. You cannot just talk about "sharing burdens" – you must actually share burdens. You cannot tell your spouse you love him or her while you treat him or her with disrespect. And, you cannot under any circumstances ignore the *Golden Rule* of life and of love – treat others as you would like them to treat you. In a successful marriage, you more often than not get what you give. Kindness, respect, the sharing of life's burdens, and being a person of integrity will be reciprocated in ways that will add to the richness and fullness of your marriage.

5. And finally, all newlyweds must understand this very simple lesson – your marriage will not always be fair, just, and beautiful! All of the best marriages have gone through tough times. All marriages have their challenges. How you build the foundation of your marriage in the early stages will go a long way towards determining whether your marriage can weather the various storms that lie ahead. Trust us on this – your marriage will be challenged along the way. One of you will lose a job. A family member will get very ill. A child might die. One of you will be transferred to another job location. There will be times when you wonder whether you can make it to the next day of your life. Your marriage will be challenged in ways you never imagined. It happens. Expect it. The good news, all of the most successful marriages have survived the ups and downs, and yours can as well.

All marriages go through seasons - much like the seasons of nature. Marriage is born in the Spring, blossoms over the Summer, grows to maturity in the Fall, and settles in over the Winter. When we find true love, most of us find it for a lifetime. Those marriages and relationships that last over time started with the simple planting of a seed. The seed was nourished over time. Love grown with tender and loving care matures into fully-grown love that can withstand the tests of time.

We have learned a lot about what makes marriages work over these past 26 years. If you heed the advice of all those successfully married couples we have interviewed across the globe, you will have a good chance of making your marriage work – of making it not only survive, but thrive. You've had a perfect wedding and now you have a glimpse of what can come next if only you will commit to these simple notions. Start today.

WHAT IS LOVE?

SIMPLE THINGS MATTER

CHAPTER 1

Summer Love

The truth is, if we all had our Summer of Love there would be no violence, no heartbreak, no disaffection, no scorn or hate—there would be only love and peace.

THERE IS SOMETHING ABOUT the summer that encourages love. Maybe it's the bright summer sun. It could be the warm summer breeze. Maybe it's the refreshing summer water! Perhaps, it is the summer vacation. And isn't baseball played mostly in the summer?

Whatever the cause, it appears that most people fall in love during the summer and get married during the summer – more than in any other season of the year. In fact, the research data we have collected over the years reveals that the months of June, July, August, and September are the most popular months to get married. Needless to say, we have often wondered why. Why all this Summer Love?

Recently, we came upon a statement by Simran Khurana that we just love. It goes like this: "Summer has always been considered to be the most romantic of the four seasons. The clear skies, the blazing sun, the gentle summer breeze, and the lazy afternoons flavor the season with passion and warm love."

We think Simran has it right. Summer is the most romantic of the four seasons. The seed of love is planted in the spring, and when it is properly nurtured, it will blossom in the summer. Love can be felt in every corner of the world during the warm summer months. Couples just seem to appear everywhere – holding hands, wrapping each other in hugs, exchanging kisses and fondly gazing into each other's eyes. Ah, the Summer of Love – there is nothing like it!

"Love is to the heart what the summer is to the farmer's year – it brings to harvest all the loveliest flowers of the soul." We don't know the source of this quote but we refer to it often when talking about Summer Love. We are particularly captivated by the notion of harvesting "the loveliest flowers of the soul." Here's what we think it means.

When Charley was a child, he always marveled at the bountiful harvest his grandparents, uncles, and aunts were capable of bringing forth in the fall of the year. Wheat was beautiful and golden. The corn was ten feet high! The crops they planted and harvested in the rich bottomlands along the Missouri River were simply amazing. But why, he would often ask? What's so special about this place? Charley quickly learned the answer.

Crops planted in the spring and nourished by the rains grew to gargantuan proportions in the rich soil along the river. And by the end of summer, the crops grew tall, they grew healthy, and they were ripe for the harvest.

Summer Love shares all of these characteristics. Love springs eternal in the spring and is nourished by the rain. But always remember, it grows under the warm sun of summer! Love comes to fruition in the summer. It grows to gargantuan proportions. Summer makes love ripe for the harvest. Summer is the season of love. It is the Summer of Love.

Life is fragile. Life is uncertain. Life is not forever. Love today. Hug someone tonight. In love and life, there is nothing more important than having someone to love, and someone who loves you. Enjoy your Summer of Love.

Being in love – there is nothing like it. There is nothing that can trump it. There is nothing more important in life than finding someone to love – someone to truly love.

The truth is, if we all had our Summer of Love there would be no violence, no heartbreak, no disaffection, no scorn or hate – there would be only love and peace.

Go be in love. There is nothing like it!

C H A P T E R 2

Lessons of Love from Your Dog

Over the years, we have learned much about the essentials of a loving relationship by observing our dog, Jake.

WE ARE PROUD TO TELL you that Jake is truly a Wonder Dog. He is loving, caring, intuitive, intelligent, handsome, and a wonderful friend and companion. Frankly, we love him like a child. And the good news is, he loves us right back! And he loves us unconditionally!

Jake is a mixed breed dog – half Golden Retriever and half Yellow Lab. He is a marvelous dog. He is a beautiful dog. He has been our faithful companion and best friend for nearly 13 years. He is everything you could ever want in a best friend. He tells us by his "words" and his actions that he is delighted to see us, that he missed us, and that he loves us. And when we come home from work he shivers, howls a gurgling sound, and wags his tail uncontrollably.

No matter how bad our day, no matter how stressful our work, and no matter how tired we are, just seeing Jake lifts up our spirits, relaxes us, and makes us feel loved. Isn't that amazing? How can a dog have that effect upon us? How can our Wonder Dog, Jake, make us forget all of our cares and woes, lift up our spirits so completely, and make us feel so warm and fuzzy?

Here's the first lesson. Our dog loves us unconditionally. He doesn't love us "If we do something he likes," "If we feed him his food and water," "If we let him sleep with us in bed," "If we comb his fur," or "If we take him to the Vet." He just loves us. He loves us unconditionally. People in the human race should learn this simple lesson.

Secondly, Jake never lies to us. He always tells us the truth. When those soft brown eyes look at you, you melt! There is no equivocation in his eyes. He loves us, plain and simple. Just tell the truth! The eyes know love.

Thirdly, Jake never bites us. Oh, for sure, he might let out a little growl when you try to move him over so you can get in bed, but that is only a warning that he has found his "cozy place" in bed and you are intruding on his space. But bite? Never in a thousand years. He disagrees with us from time to time, but we are his friends, his family, and his supporters. To bite us is so far from his mind that he could never imagine it. And neither could we.

And finally, Jake knows the most important lesson of all – we are his best friends, his family, his trusted associates, and his providers. He can count on us through thick and thin. He can count on us when the chips are down. Jake knows in his heart that we would never let him down, never cheat on him, never hurt him, and never betray him. He loves us unconditionally and we love him just the same.

You can learn a lot about love from a dog. Our Wonder Dog Jake has taught us the loving lessons of life. We are eternally grateful for his love, his trust, and his companionship.

To learn the lessons we have learned from Jake is to have learned the essence of love. Jake has inspired us on to even greater love. We owe the big boy! His example about love is a model we should all follow. Human beings could learn a lot about love from Jake. Thanks, Jake. We love you unconditionally.

CHAPTER 3

You Are Always in My Heart

Couple after couple report to us how they always think about the one they love when they are in the room next door or when they are on the other side of world.

RECENTLY, WE DISCOVERED a new singing group called *Pink Martini.* Our daughter put us on to this group several weeks ago so we downloaded them from iTunes. We have been grooving to their sounds ever since! They are utterly delightful and we highly recommend them to you as we have to many others. They reside in Portland, Oregon.

Pink Martini's music is unique and highly enjoyable and they often have songs on the same album sung in a variety of languages including French, Spanish, English, and Italian. They have also recorded songs for their albums in Croatian, Japanese, Portuguese,

Arabic, and other languages. Their group as one reviewer said, "Essentially plays internationalist orchestral pop that is a model of taste and restraint." We describe their music to friends as jazzy music, as toe-tapping music with Latin rhythms and overtones of classical and pop. Blended together a musical sound is created that is very unique and smashingly lovely.

One of the songs on their album *Hey Eugene!* is called *Everywhere* and we think it has important lessons about love and relationships. One verse goes like this: "Every time I'm far from home I am never quite alone. Whenever we're apart you're always in my heart. For you are with me everywhere."

We have heard a similar refrain from many, many of the couples we have interviewed. Couple after couple report to us how they always think about the one they love when they are in the room next door or when they are on the other side of world. They talk about feeling almost as if the person they love more that anyone or anything else in the world is part of them wherever they are. It's like their lover has become a physical and psychological part of who they are.

A friend of ours has recently fallen in love and reports that he thinks of his new lady "all the time!" To us, this phenomenon is one of the best indicators of real love. Not only do you think about the person you love nearly all the time but you feel their presence in your heart and in your soul. You feel as if they are a part of you. You are constantly pre-occupied with them. You are in love!

For more answers to the question "How will I know I am in love" you might want to read the section of this book answering that question. When you recognize that you are truly in love, you are ready to enjoy seeing love in every corner of the world.

Another stanza from the song, *Everywhere*, sums this notion all up we think. It goes like this – "Everywhere I go I see a world designed for you and me. I always realize, with every new sunrise, that you are with me everywhere."

To feel this way is to feel love and to be in love. Trust the way you feel. Believe in love. Believe in true love because to feel this way is to have love in your heart. To feel this way about another human being is to look forward to sunrises that awaken every day within you the realization that you love someone else more that yourself.

Being in love is wonderful. Being in love for a lifetime is heaven. "You are always in my heart" is a refrain you feel for someone because you are in love. And who knows, someday you may celebrate your golden anniversary together.

CHAPTER 4

Fully-Grown Love Never Fails

Love is patient, love is kind.
It does not envy, it does not boast, it is not proud
It is not rude, it is not self-seeking.
It is not easily angered, it keeps no record of wrongs.
Love does not delight in evil, but rejoices with the truth.
It always protects, always trusts,
always hopes, always perseveres.
Love never fails. (I Corinthians 13:4-8)

As we sit at our desk today we are listening to a gentle rain. Spring is only a few days away. You can smell it in the air. You can see it. After several months of winter you look forward to the pretty flowers, the budding trees, and the gentle springing to life of nature. You see it all around you. Hope springs eternal in the Spring and it makes you feel good. It always reminds us of what is truly important in life and in love.

And the birds seem to be looking forward to it as they are frolicking around the backyard trees in search, it seems, of other birds to hang around with. Maybe they are looking for love. They surely will find it today. Spring has sprung!

We have always felt that Spring, in so many ways, is a great metaphor for the evolution of true love. You start with a gentle rain and the seeds of love you planted start to grow until some day the love is real and fully-grown. Nature has a wonderful way of making us reflect on our life, our love, and all the good that surrounds us. Spring reminds us that fully-grown love never fails.

The amazing thing about fully-grown true love is that it adds so much to your life and to the life of the one you love. And interestingly enough we have found the quote from the Bible (I Corinthians 13:4-8) to be awfully apropos as a way of describing all of the successfully married couples we have interviewed over the years. Irrespective of your spiritual persuasion, these words written so long ago still apply today. Successfully married couples engage in fully-grown love and we believe this passage describes such love in all the right ways.

As we have often said, all marriages go through seasons – much like the seasons of nature. It is born in the Spring, blossoms over the Summer, grows to maturity in the Fall, and settles in over the Winter. When we find true love, most of us find it for a lifetime. We find it for the four seasons of life. Those marriages and relationships that last over time started with the simple planting of a seed. The seed was nourished over time. Love grown with tender loving care matures into fully-grown love that can withstand the tests of time.

Fully-grown love never fails and to hear the refrain tells us why.

Love is patient, love is kind.
It does not envy, it does not boast, it is not proud.
It is not rude, it is not self-seeking.
It is not easily angered, it keeps no record of wrongs.
Love does not delight in evil, but rejoices with the truth.
It always protects, always trusts,
always hopes, always perseveres.
Love never fails. (I Corinthians 13:4-8).

Enjoy love. Enjoy life. Relish the seasons. Love never fails.

C H A P T E R 5

Love's Essential Virtues

We would offer that gratitude is the secret of a successful loving relationship.

THIS MORNING, A GREAT FRIEND of ours sent along an article that we were really taken with. The article was by Dr. Tom Lickona based upon his book entitled *Character Matters: How to Help our Children Develop Good Judgment, Integrity, and Other Essential Virtues* (Simon & Schuster, ©2004). We were struck by the similarity of the "virtues" he believes essential for "strong character" and the virtues we have discovered in our research over the years about successful loving relationships.

The first essential virtue highlighted by Dr. Lickona is "wisdom." According to Tom, wisdom is the master virtue that directs all others. Wisdom "tells us how to put the other virtues into practice – when to act, how to act, and how to balance different virtues when they conflict" such as "telling the honest truth" even when it "might hurt someone's feelings." We refer to this notion often in our book when we speak of the importance of honesty in our relationships with those we love.

The second virtue is justice according to Dr. Lickona. "Justice means respecting the rights of all persons." In our book, we refer to this virtue as the Golden Rule – do unto others as you would have them do unto you.

The third virtue is "fortitude." According to Lickona, "fortitude enables us to do what is right in the face of difficulty." Or, more succinctly, doing the "hard right instead of the easy wrong." As we discuss in our book, all successful loving relationships have hard times, great challenges, and failures. More importantly, however, those whose love lasts a lifetime have overcome the challenges in life and have been strengthened by them. Overcoming these challenges together makes for a stronger and even more loving relationship. Fortitude is the strength to carry on even when we find it hard in our relationships to see the light at the end of the tunnel.

"Self-Control" is the fourth virtue. In its simplest terms, "self-control is the ability and the strength to govern ourselves – to control our temper and to regulate our appetites and passions." It is as Lickona says, the "power to resist temptation." All marriages and loving relationships have their temptations. Trust us on that. The successful ones don't act on their temptations; hence, they survive and thrive.

The fifth virtue according to Lickona is "love" – "the willingness to sacrifice for the sake of another." Successful loving relationships quickly learn that their relationship is not about "you" or "me." It is about "we" and "us." This is a critical factor in successful relationships. Suffice it to say, people who are truly in love do not spend their time finding fault with each other – they do not spend their time putting down or belittling each other. They find strength in the virtues of each other. They love each other in the truest sense of the word.

As the purveyors of positive love, we really like Lickona's sixth virtue – "positive attitude." We once heard a speaker say, "If you frown, you frown alone, but a smile is infectious!" Maintaining a positive attitude is a great virtue. Who wants to be around negative people? Successful loving relationships work like this as well. If your spouse or your lover is always in a negative mood you will work hard not to be around them. The choice of being negative or positive is ours. Choose positive!

Hard work is the "seventh indispensable virtue" according to Lickona. If you want to be successful in love and life you must work hard. Nothing worth having in a relationship comes easy. You must earn it. Love is something you earn. As we say all the time, the simple things required to make love work take lots of hard work, day in and day out, throughout the life of the loving relationship.

Our favorite virtue is "integrity." As Lickona says, "Integrity is adhering to moral principle, being faithful to moral conscience, keeping your word, and standing up for what we believe." In love and marriage, you don't cheat on the one you love! You don't lie to the one you love. You are faithful to the one you love. There are no exceptions to this basic virtue. To truly love someone is to tell the truth to them and to yourself.

Dr. Lickona reminds us that "Gratitude is often described as the secret of a happy life." We would offer that gratitude is the secret of a successful loving relationship. We must show gratitude for the one we purport to love. We should always take the time to thank those we love for their support, their understanding, their sacrifice for us, and for their love. Always show your gratitude to the one you love. They will love you for it!

And finally, the tenth virtue according to Dr. Lickona is "humility." Humility "makes us aware of our imperfections and leads us to become a better person." And as in love and marriage, "humility enables us to take responsibility for our faults and failings (rather than blaming someone else), apologize for them and seek to make amends." To be truly in love, in our opinion, requires us to recognize that we are not the center of the universe – that the world does not revolve around us. People who are truly in love, learn from each other, they respect each other, they value each other, and they recognize that in the best loving relationships, personal humility allows us to understand the simple notion that trying to prove you are right when you are clearly wrong, is not a virtue. Trying to win a senseless and pointless argument is not a virtue. It is good to be humble!

We would encourage you to read more of Dr. Lickona's work and you will see as we do that his "essential virtues" are, in many ways, a mirror of our "seven secrets of a successful marriage."

CHAPTER 6

Seasons of Baseball and Love

Over the years we have marveled at the parallels between the seasons of the year, and baseball and love.

SPRING HAS SPRING! IN THE Spring, all things are possible, every team can win the Pennant, and love is born! In so many ways, Spring is a metaphor for love, and hope, and the boundless promise of the dawn of a new season. In so many ways, the game of baseball speaks to all of these. And lest you think we are baseball fans – we are!

First, do you remember that old familiar song, "Take me out to the ball game?" According to some reputable sources it is the third most sung song in America. One and two are "Happy Birthday" and "The Star Spangled Banner," respectively. We can find no evidence to dispute this notion.

And while most people are familiar with the chorus, almost no one has heard the rest of the popular song written by Jack Norworth in 1908 and revised in 1927. We have quoted the rest of the song below from the 1927 version.

Nelly Kelly loved baseball games,
Knew the players, knew all their names.
You could see her there ev'ry day,
Shout "Hurray" when they'd play.
Her boyfriend by the name of Joe
Said, "To Coney Isle, dear, let's go,"
Then Nelly started to fret and pout,
And to him, I heard her shout:

Chorus
"Take me out to the ball game,
Take me out on to the crowds;
Buy me some peanuts and Cracker Jacks,
I don't care if I never get back.
Let me root, root, root for the home team,
If they don't win, it's a shame.
For it's one, two, three strikes, you're out,
At the old ball game."

Nelly Kelly was in love with Joe. But being the independent minded women she apparently was, she told Joe she would rather go to a baseball game with him than join him for a day at Coney Island in New York City.

For those of you who may not know, Coney Island is a neighborhood in the Big Apple and it is home to one of the most well-known and longest running amusement parks in the United States. During the summer, in particular, lovers flock to Coney Island for roller coaster rides, cotton candy, hot dogs, and romance. It is a destination for lovers both young and old. You can lose all of your cares and woes at Coney Island, if only for a day. A lot of budding romances have taken seed at Coney Island, that's for sure. But Nelly Kelly it seems found love in the Spring at the baseball park. More on this notion a little later.

As a metaphor for love, the seasons of the year speak to love in all the right ways. The seed of love is planted in the Spring, begins to grow as it is nourished by April showers. It blossoms into a beautiful flower in May. It is nurtured through the Spring and Summer, matures in the Fall, and settles in for Winter. Love has its seasons. Love has its Spring of birth, its Summer of love, its Fall of maturity, and its Winter of warmth by a crackling fireplace. Love is a many splendored thing. Love is a many seasoned thing.

Now we come to baseball. Ever notice how baseball fans become convinced in the Spring that this is the year their team is going to win the World Series. Optimism abounds. On Opening Day all things seem possible. The grass is dark green and freshly manicured, the stadium is squeaky clean, the smell of great food permeates the air, and the crack of the bat is a sound you have missed for far too long. When baseball season begins in the Spring, life begins again for young and old alike. Baseball begins in Spring for a reason! And so does love.

Over the years we have marveled at the parallels between the seasons of the year, and baseball and love. Nelly Kelly certainly had it right – "Take me out to the ballgame." She had it all – someone to love, her favorite game, and the seasons of love, life, and baseball to enjoy. May you enjoy your seasons of baseball and love as we have.

C H A P T E R 7

Love Is Like Learning To Dance

It is like watching a pair of ice dancers gliding through a perfectly executed lift – they are beautiful skaters individually, but magnificent when together.

IN OUR AWARD WINNING BOOK, *Golden Anniversaries: The Seven Secrets of Successful Marriage*, we describe the seven pervasive characteristics present in all successful marriages – and we would dare say, in all successful and loving relationships between two people. We often use the notion of "learning to dance" as a way of describing these relationships. Dance becomes a metaphor for successful love.

You have probably heard the expression, "It takes two to Tango." When we were in Buenos Aires, Argentina a couple of years ago, this point was really driven home to us as we watched the Tango dancers perform on the streets. Tango dancing is exotic, breathtaking, sexy, exhilarating, entertaining, heart-pumping, and just plain fun. But here is one absolute fact – you cannot do the Tango by yourself! It does, indeed, take two to Tango.

The characteristics we describe are a pervasive part of who loving couples are ***together*** as if describing the steps of a well-choreographed dance. Successful couples have learned, practiced and committed these characteristics to memory. It is like watching a pair of ice dancers gliding through a perfectly executed lift – they are beautiful skaters individually, but magnificent when together.

On the other hand, failed marriages and failed relationships are like dancing in the dark without knowing the steps. The steps appear to be easy at first, but tragically, divorce statistics tell us that too many married couples never learn to dance. Instead, they stumble and fall until they eventually give up and quit dancing altogether. If they had learned to make the seven characteristics part of the fabric of their marriage, the fabric of their loving relationship, they could have learned the dance of lasting love.

If you want to achieve a lasting love, first learn and understand that the simple things matter in love and marriage. Then accept the commitment to do the simple things everyday of your loving relationship. While it might seem easy at first glance, successful couples describe the hard work it takes to make doing the simple things habitual and pervasive in their relationship.

Learning to dance is fun, but it is also hard work. It takes commitment to perfect the moves. Remember, successful relationships are, more than anything, an accumulation of the simple things. To use the Tango dance as an example, in a holistic sense it is beautiful to watch, but the beauty of the dance is made possible because those doing the dance did the simple things – they learned the steps, and they practiced a lot!

Whether the beat of your loving relationship is a Tango, Salsa, Swing, Waltz, or the Texas Two-Step, when each of these seven characteristics describes your dance together, you will have achieved a successful loving relationship with another person. You will then be well on your way to achieving a long-lasting love like the successful couples we have interviewed over the years who celebrated their Golden Anniversaries together.

Love is like learning to dance. Learn how today. And as a good friend of ours in Texas likes to say, "You meet a lot of nice people when you go dancing!"

CHAPTER 8

Is Love a Second Hand Emotion?

Falling in love is so very human.
When you feel it in your
heart and in your soul,
take the chance – take the risk.

WHAT'S LOVE GOT TO DO with it? Is love really a second hand emotion? A famous song focused on these notions. So what's the truth about love? Is it real or is it a second hand emotion?

The truth is, love is something very hard to define. Love is often times indescribable. And most certainly, love is NOT a second hand emotion. There is no question about it – love is real! Love is something you feel. Love is something you know to be true even if you can't define it or describe it.

Over the years we have talked to thousands of people in love, about love. We have discovered the truths about "How you know you are in love," "The secrets of successful love," and "How to sustain love." And through it all, we know these truths to be self-evident – love is real, love is definable, and love is sustainable, often throughout a lifetime.

One of the icons of the entertainment business, Tina Turner, wrote a very popular song entitled, *What's Love Got to Do with It?* Our favorite verse of the lyrics of this St. Louis Walk of Fame inductee goes like this:

Oh, what's love got to do with it
What's love but a second hand emotion
What's love got to do with it
Who needs a heart
When a heart can be broken

Tina had it right in many ways. Love can be scary. Love can be cruel. Love can, for sure, be something that confuses you. It can be, in the end, something that breaks your heart. All this is true, but here's where we part ways with Tina's lyrics – even though love stands a chance of turning out badly and breaking your heart, to fall in love and to be in love is a risk in life that is well worth taking, irrespective of the chances of failure.

Frankly, it is natural to be afraid of falling in love. But to fall in love is something that is uniquely human. It is an emotion that often confuses people who think they are in love, but in the end, being in love is a wonderful emotion – an emotion that is exhilarating to feel. And only humans can feel it!

Only a human heart can be broken. To truly be in love, however, is to take the chance that your heart might, in the end, be broken. But can you imagine what you lose by not taking the chance to fall in love?

Love is something you feel. Love is something you feel in your heart. And love is totally worth the risk. Love is NOT a second hand emotion; it is the most exhilarating emotion that all human beings will feel in their lifetime. Go for it!

Falling in love is so very human. When you feel it in your heart and in your soul, take the chance – take the risk. Sure, your heart can be broken, but can you imagine going through life without loving another human being in the deepest and most intimate way?

Being in love is worth the risk. Love is NOT a second hand emotion!

CHAPTER 9

A Sypmphony of Love

Music has a way to touch your heartstrings.
It has a way to make your heart sing.

TONIGHT, WE HEARD THE SOUNDS of love! Over the years we have seen love, felt love, heard about love, observed love, and been in love. But tonight, we heard the sounds of love!

We heard love tonight through the magnificent sounds of the St. Louis Symphony Orchestra (SLSO), the second oldest symphony orchestra in the United States of America. David Robertson joined the SLSO as its conductor several years ago after a highly successful tenure as Conductor in Lyon, France. The Maestro is incredibly energetic and the audience loves his passion, emotion, and enthusiasm for his work. The audience tonight, as on all nights, adored the Maestro and the Orchestra during the concert, and the feeling was clearly reciprocated by them.

The concert we watched was their Carnegie Hall Preview Concert. As usual, their actual Carnegie Hall concert a few days later received wonderful reviews from the New York critics! Their renditions of Wagner and Sibelius were especially stirring and breathtaking.

But how you say does this have anything to do with love and marriage? Our response – it has everything to do with love and marriage! The beautiful sounds we heard tonight were about joy. They were inspiring. They were heart pounding. They gave you cold chills. They made you feel good all over. They sounds we heard from this magnificent orchestra tonight were the sounds of love. The reciprocal relationship between orchestra and conductor was a clear demonstration of the power of love. Much like a successful marriage.

Music has a way to touch your heartstrings. It has a way to make your heart sing. Music, perhaps more than anything else, has a way to magically transform your body and soul to a place of love, peace, and serenity. Tonight, we heard the sounds of love. We experienced the throbbing pulse you feel every time the someone you love walks into the room and into your life.

For many years, we have viewed a symphony orchestra as a metaphor for successful love and marriage. Every player has a part to play. No one player is more important than the other. Each person playing an instrument must play his or her part. When one doesn't, or when they play it badly, the music written by the composer suffers. Beautiful sounds become noise. Harmonic structures sound like fingernails on a chalkboard. But when each player plays his or her part to perfection, you hear lovely and breathtaking music, like we did tonight.

Which brings us to the point of all this. Tonight at the SLSO concert we experienced a special moment. We saw a house full of people at magnificent Powell Symphony Hall in St. Louis, Missouri fall in love tonight. The conductor was extraordinary, the orchestra played wonderfully, and the audience responded with love, affection, and admiration for both. Love was in the air. You could feel it. You could sense it. You could hear it.

Following the final standing ovation, exultation and joy were present everywhere. It was like love. It was amazing. We heard the sounds of love tonight and it felt good.

So for you lovers out there, here is the "Doctors List" of the Top 20 Symphony Orchestras in the United States. We compiled this list after reviewing many, many sources. And we know, some will quibble over our list, and we encourage that! The truth is, we want you to experience the joy with your favorite orchestra that we experienced with ours tonight and all those other nights throughout the year.

Here they are, "The Doctors Top 20" --

1) Chicago Symphony Orchestra
2) Cleveland Orchestra
3) Los Angeles Philharmonic
4) Boston Symphony Orchestra
5) New York Philharmonic
6) Saint Louis Symphony Orchestra
7) San Francisco Symphony
8) Minnesota Orchestra
9) Philadelphia Orchestra
10) Cincinnati Symphony
11) Pittsburgh Symphony
12) Atlanta Symphony
13) Houston Symphony
14) National Symphony (Washington, DC)

15) Miami New World Symphony
16) Dallas Symphony
17) Seattle Symphony
18) Baltimore Symphony
19) Detroit Symphony Orchestra
20) Colorado Symphony Orchestra

One final reminder – Conductor David Robertson and his wife, Orli Shaham, have a beautiful marriage. We are sure their marriage would parallel very closely the many successfully married couples we have interviewed over the past quarter century across cultures, countries, and continents. Come to think of it, when the Maestro and the SLSO play their beautiful music, they are probably expressing the beautiful sounds of David and Orli's marriage – a symphony of love and marriage!

CHAPTER 10

Real Love Is Colorblind

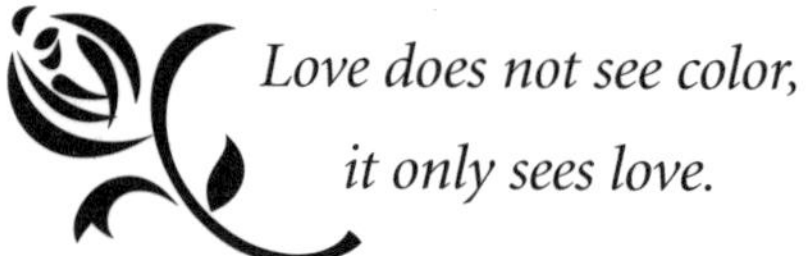

THE ROMANTIC 1955 MOVIE, *Love is a Many Splendored Thing*, tells the story of an American reporter who falls in love with a Eurasian doctor. And as you might have guessed, they encounter prejudice from both of their families. Such prejudice was, unfortunately, all too common in 1955. It is all too common in 2009.

People in love, it seems, do not always find a colorblind world. That's too bad. Love is love. People who are in love, love each other irrespective of their race, creed, color, or national origin. True love between two people is colorblind – never forget that! Love does not see color, it only sees love.

In our research and travels we have often encountered people in love who have suffered the "slings and arrows of misfortune" because their relationship was a bi-racial one, or in many cases, a multi-racial relationship. Often times, there are people who observe others in love, but they do not always just see love. They see race. They see people who are different. Their prejudices take over. The dark side of some takes over. Too bad.

During the film, Love is a Many Splendored Thing, some intensely romantic meetings occur on a high and windswept hill. The song lyrics are clearly audible during many parts of the film.

This intensely romantic song touches the heart. It touched our heart. It will touch yours. It goes like this:

Once on a high and windy hill,
In the morning mist, two lovers kissed,
And the world stood still.

You see, two people in love know their love for each other is timeless. They know their love is unconditional. They know it transcends everything else, even prejudice. Love between two people who are truly in love trumps everything else.

There is another line from the song that we think is particularly lovely:

Love is nature's way of giving.
A reason to be living.

Love must be shared. Love must be enjoyed. Love, quite frankly, is nature's way of telling people in love that they have many reasons to live – that they have many reasons to spend their life with the one they love.

There is another message about love. Love, when it comes your way, must be embraced. When you fall in love, you must seize the moment. Love does not always wait. When you fall in love, when you feel it completely, you must seize the moment:

Love is a many splendored thing
It's the April rose that only grows in the early spring.

When you fall in love, when you fall deeply in love, there is a good chance it will be forever. True love is between two individuals who see only love when they gaze into each other's eyes. Those in love do not see race, color, national origin, or prejudice. They see only love.

Love is a many splendored thing. Love is colorblind to those in love, and it should be to those who observe those in love.

CHAPTER 11

Nicknames: The Private Code for Love

Nicknames are a private code for saying, "I Love You."

OVER OUR 42 YEARS OF marriage we have met thousands of couples that deeply loved each other. Nearly every one of them had an affectionate nickname for each other – a sort of private "code" for saying, "I love you."

Some of the nicknames are ones you have probably heard many times before – "lovey-dovey," "sweetie-pie," "sugar," "snookie-poo," "honey," "darling," "sweetness," "sweetpea," "baby girl," "lover boy," "sunshine," "sugarplum," "baby-doll," "hey, handsome," "hey, beautiful," and so forth.

Some of the nicknames are unusual and funny. Names like "Butch" in reference to a very petite wife seem unusual, but to her husband, it is an endearing term. "Snookems," in reference to a very manly-man does not compute with most people, but to his wife, the term is an expression of love and affection. And the list goes on.

Over the years, the funniest "affectionate" nickname we ever heard was from the wife who lovingly referred to her husband as, "turkey-fart." It is not important to understand the origin of "turkey-fart." What is important is that the name has special meaning to the husband and wife team that coined it. You see, love has a private code. People in love understand! Nicknames are a private code for saying, "I Love You."

CHAPTER 12

What Is Love?

In the end, to understand true love you must go with your heart.

WHAT IS THIS THING CALLED love? Let us count the ways.

There is platonic love, erotic love, family love, puppy love, romantic love, unrequited love, sexual love, virtuous love, and just plain love! Love comes in many forms and varieties. But one thing is certain – people in love know love, feel love, experience love, and practice love.

But what is this thing called love? Through time immemorial people have been trying to define love, understand love, feel love, and practice love. Yet, in the end, most would agree that love is something you feel – you feel in your heart and in your emotions. You can't define it. You can only experience it.

Throughout time, men and women have wondered about love, wrote about love, talked about love, and experienced love. Many have said the obvious – "I can't define love but I know it when I feel it!"

One thing is certain – those who try to define love as something scientific miss the essential points about love. Love is not chemical, psychological, religious, or physiological. It is all of these! But in the end, love is something you feel. It is something you feel first in your heart and then in your head. Love is compassionate, arousing, uplifting, and it is truly human.

Throughout the millennia, much has been written about love. Paul Frances Webster wrote:

Love is a many splendored thing
It's the April rose that only grows in the early spring

Beautiful, huh? And the poem (later a popular song) illustrates the simplicity of love. Love is something you feel. You can't describe it in ways that give it justice. You can wax on eloquently about its meaning, but in the end it is almost indescribable. But without a doubt, love is a many splendored thing.

The truth about love is the following – true love, real love, and unrequited love cannot be defined. True love can only be felt.

True love is an emotion. True love is a feeling you have for another human being that is different from the love you have ever felt for another human being.

In the end, to understand true love you must go with your heart. Don't make love so complicated. Don't make love indefinable. In the end, understand love by – how you feel in your heart.

In the end, love matters. Go with the flow. Love someone for life. Love someone deeply. Love someone intimately. Love someone for you, and for them. There is nothing like it.

HOW CAN I FIND LOVE?

SIMPLE THINGS MATTER

CHAPTER 13

Happily Ever After: It Can Happen To You!

Fairy tales do come true,
in life and in love.
It can happen to you.

WE SAW AN ENCHANTING movie today. It reminded us again that people fall in love and stay in love for a lifetime. Fairy tales do come true, in life and in love. It can happen to you. You can live happily ever after.

The movie we saw was entitled, *Enchanted.* It lived up to its title. It was enticing, engaging, bewitching, fascinating, charming and delightful – just like your heart feels when you are in love. The movie was a reflection of true love for many in love, and it reminds you that sometimes, suddenly and out of nowhere, you fall in love! And it also reminds you that sometimes you thought you loved someone else, only to discover that it was really another that captured your heart. Following what your heart tells you is the only path to true love.

It is our sincere belief that people have an innate need to love and to be in love. Some of us spend time searching for love endlessly and never find it. Others amongst us search for love, find it, and then discover that it was not true love. And still others search for love and find it – and it lasts a lifetime. These are the ones who fall in love "happily ever after."

There is another category of love – those who did not seek it, but suddenly, and out of nowhere, find themselves in love! They didn't go looking for it but they found it nonetheless. But love has a way of finding people from time to time and when that happens – look out! Sparks fly, fireworks go off, the moon shines brighter, and the human heart pounds out a tune that says, I am in love! I am in love! I am in love! They don't know what hit them. They are smitten by love. They have what we like to call, "Enchanted Love."

You will recall similar stories where the glass slipper fits the foot of the lovely maiden just before the stroke of midnight. Well, the movie *Enchanted* does not disappoint. In the end, the glass slipper fits a lovely lady and all is well with the world. All is well with love. Fairy tales do come true in life and love It can happen to you! And when it does it is enchanting!

True love works this way as well. Sometimes, you become convinced that true love will never come your way. You search the world over, but alas, true love for you is elusive. It hides from you. It disguises itself as love, but it proves to be only an imitator or an imposter. And then suddenly and out of nowhere, you are in love! You have enchanted love. You have lasting love.

We worry from time to time that people today do not believe that love with someone else can last a lifetime. But you know what, it can. And it does. People fall in love and the love they share lasts forever. People in love really do live happily ever after. Of that you can be sure.

Frankly, we have grown weary of the so-called "experts" who believe that love and marriage is old fashioned. We are tired of the prognosticators who proclaim daily that love for a single person that lasts a lifetime is not possible anymore. In our research throughout the USA and around the world we have seen too much evidence to the contrary. The successfully married couples we interviewed over the past three decades say the same things as the successfully married couples we interview today. True love crosses the generational barriers.

When you fall in love, truly fall in love, you feel it in your heart and in your soul. The feelings are unmistakable. They are undeniable. Real love is not a secret. Real love does not disguise itself. Real love can last forever. And contrary to the naysayers too prevalent in our society today, most people truly in love share that love for a lifetime. They do, indeed, live happily ever after.

Fairy tales do come true in life and love. It can happen to you.

CHAPTER 14

Why Is Love Blind?

What you feel in your heart
does not need eyes to see.

THE PHRASE, "LOVE IS BLIND," most likely originated in the Shakespeare play, the *Merchant of Venice.* In the play the character Jessica says the following:

I am glad 'tis night, you do not look on me,
For I am much ashamed of my exchange:
But love is blind and lovers cannot see
The pretty follies that themselves commit;
For if they could, Cupid himself would blush
To see me thus transformed to a boy.

And now it seems, science has proved that Shakespeare had it right! Love is, indeed, blind.

Scientists at University College London reported in the journal, *NeuroImage,* that romantic love suppresses "neural activity associated with critical social assessment of other people and negative emotions." It seems that once we get close to another person --once we fall in love with them – our brain has a reduced need to assess their character and to harbor negative emotions towards them. Our love for them is blind. It is love we feel. It is not love we see.

It is our profound belief that the notion of "love is blind" has much merit. It is nature's way of allowing us to express our love for another person because we feel that love for them in our heart and in our soul. Our feelings of love are unconditional at the point we express them. Romantic love is often blind, but that is not a bad thing.

Here is our twist on this intriguing notion. When you kiss someone you love in a romantic way, do you keep your eyes open or shut? Our bet – you close your eyes. Isn't this the essence of "love is blind?" You do not have to see the one you love to know you love them. You accept it on blind faith. And you kiss them without fear, without any sense of danger. You love them, if you will, blindly.

Over the years, we have interviewed thousands of couples who were in love. We have found many, many common characteristics that were pervasive throughout these loving relationships. Most notably, however, those in love, those truly in love, had love that transcended anything you could see or touch with your hand. Their love was love based on trust. Their love was unconditional love. Their love, if you will, was love based on feelings that were heart-felt. Their love was so strong and so deep, it had become blind love.

It is okay to express your love openly, freely, unequivocally, honestly, and yes, blindly. What you feel in your heart does not need eyes to see.

CHAPTER 15

Looking for Love In All The Wrong Places

In our judgment, one of the principle causes for multiple divorce is because people in search of love look for it in all the wrong places.

YOU OFTEN HEAR THAT 50% of marriages in the United States end in divorce. While technically correct, that number does not tell the whole story. As a professor friend of ours used to say, "Statistics are for liars and damn liars!" The harsh reality is, people can take the same numbers and draw different meanings. Let's take a deeper look at this phenomenon and try to determine a number that is probably more accurate – one that more honestly reflects the real truth about marriage for most people.

The first simple truth is that there are a lot of people who get married multiple times. The record shows that there are people who have actually been married six or more times. Just imagine, being married six or more times! We suspect that this is because they are, in part, looking for love in all the wrong places

The second simple truth is that somewhere between 35% and 40% of first marriages end in divorce. But here is where it gets interesting—those getting divorced from their first marriage who remarry are much more likely to get divorced a second time. The USA divorce rate after the second marriage ranges from 60% to 67%, depending on whose numbers you believe. But the real eye-opening number is that nearly 75% of third marriages end in divorce!

So, what does one conclude from all this? First, the divorce rate in the USA impacts far fewer individuals than you have probably been led to believe by the popular media. Second, the actual number of people effected by divorce is probably much lower than 50% if you remove from the equation those who have been divorced more than once.

So what's up with the high number of people getting married and divorced multiple times? There is science involved with understanding why so many marriages beyond the first one fail. People desperate for love go to singles bars, nightclubs, use dating services, log on to e-Harmony.com and Match.com, to name a few. Now ask yourself this very honest and forthright question – do you really expect to find Mr. Right or Ms. Right through one of these venues? That is not to say that it doesn't happen from time to time, but we suspect that people looking for true and lasting love in these places rarely find it. This is not meant as a criticism of these venues so much as our attempt to open your eyes to the chances of finding someone to spend your life with in places like this.

Frankly, the high multiple divorce rate phenomenon that affects a lot of folks is sad, really. Most people we know and have interviewed over the years really want to find true and lasting love. But our advice to them is go to places where you are more likely to find another person looking for true and lasting love – at church or the synagogue, Thanksgiving Dinner at a friend's house, over a cup of coffee while you study in the dining area at the university, at volunteer opportunities, by belonging to social organizations like dance clubs, at interest oriented meetings such as book clubs or community action groups, and at work (this gets a little complicated at times!), to name a few.

In our judgment, one of the principle causes for multiple divorce is because people in search of love look for it in all the wrong places. Start looking for love in the right places and we are confident you will find the one you want to celebrate your golden anniversary with. And if more people took this strategy, the reported divorce rate would go down dramatically and people would give marriage the chance it deserves instead of being scared away by the oft-reported negative numbers.

C H A P T E R 1 6

Marry the Right Person in the First Place

Keep your eyes wide open
when you are falling in love.
You won't regret it later.

DID YOU EVER WONDER why some people find the perfect person to marry, do so, and enjoy a love affair that lasts a lifetime? On the other hand, some marry a person that is wrong for them now, wrong for them tomorrow, and wrong for them for a lifetime? What's the difference? Why do some succeed at love and marriage where others fail?

One of our mentors, Don Clifton, the former CEO of the world renowned Gallup Organization (rest his soul), often reminded us of the power of "pervasive personality characteristics." Don defined "pervasive" as "a recurring pattern of thought and behavior." In other words, these are the personality characteristics that a human being develops within the first two decades of life that, for the most part, defines who they are for a lifetime. Don believed that you are what you are by the time you become an adult. Changing who and what you are becomes nearly impossible after that.

So what is the lesson in all this? Simple really. The people you meet in life are, by the time they reach adulthood, pretty much what they are. They won't change much, if at all. The hard truth is they can't change who they really are, even if they wanted to. Oh, sure, people as adults can make you believe from time to time that they are something different than what they really are, but in the end, they are what they are. Make no mistake about that.

When it comes to love and marriage, there is a truism that trumps all truisms. It goes like this – pay close and careful attention to the words, deeds, and actions of the person you think you are falling in love with. And in the end, pay most of your attention to their actions, first and foremost! The truth is a person's actions speak so much louder than their words. Never lose sight of this truism for to do so is to put your heart, your health, and your happiness at peril.

One of the questions we are most often asked as we travel the world discussing our work and conducting our marriage interviews is this: "What are the secrets of a successful marriage?" Our immediate answer is always the same – marry the right person!

On the surface this may seem like a flippant answer to such a serious question, but it isn't really. If people who think they are falling in love with someone would pay more attention to their actions and not the words, they wouldn't miss the telltale signs.

Here's how it works. You think you love a guy. He tells you all of the right things. But over time you begin to notice that his actions belie his words. He tells you he respects you but dismisses your opinions. He waxes on about how he puts you on a pedestal but never opens the door for you when he gets to it first. He tells you how he wants the relationship between the two of you to be a shared relationship, and then he makes all the decisions. You get the idea. We could go on.

The point is this – if you fail to notice and question the actions of the one you purport to love in the early stages of your relationship then you are deluding yourself into thinking he/she will change later on. They rarely do. And so often those that ignore the signs and the warnings end up getting married, only to discover later on that the person they married is not who they thought he/she was.

So, back to the earlier question – the best secret to a successful marriage is marrying the right person in the first place! Taking the time to carefully observe the actions of another person over a period of time tells you a lot more about them than their words ever could. All too often we hear one or both people in a marriage lament to us that if they had only paid attention to the telltale signs, they would not have married the person they married. Many of these relationships end in divorce.

We don't mean to suggest that it is always easy to tell if the one you think you love is the one you can have a successful marriage with. We do, however, believe strongly that paying close and careful attention to the one you are thinking about marrying in the early stages of your relationship can save a lot of failed marriages from happening in the first place. This is the ultimate key to a successful marriage.

If you consciously and rationally believe that the words, deeds, and actions of the one you are thinking of marrying all jive, are consistent, and match your expectations, then your marriage has half a chance at being successful.

In the end, a marriage built on this foundation has a reasonable chance of success. And while we often say that a successful marriage is an accumulation of the simple things, and that a good marriage is simple to understand, we always remind people that you have to do the simple things each and every day of your lives together to make it work.

Making a marriage a success requires hard work. If you base your marriage on a lie – you ignored the actions you were observing in the person you were falling in love with – then all of the simple things required to make a marriage work will more than likely not be enough to carry the day.

Pervasive characteristics in people are very real. They define who they are and they almost never change. As we always say, keep your eyes wide open when you are falling in love. You won't regret it later.

One final note – never enter a marriage thinking you can ignore the behaviors now and change them later. Too many have fallen prey to this notion. It rarely ever works.

CHAPTER 17

Finding Love Again

If you want to find love the second time around you must look for someone who values and cherishes the things that matter the most to you.

LET'S BE HONEST HERE - finding love the second time around is tough – it is difficult. Sometimes, it is downright painful. Oftentimes, searching for love again ends in failure. There are no magic elixirs when it comes to finding love again the second time around.

Following the death of a spouse or the loss of a spouse through divorce, many individuals are "thrown on the street again" when it comes to finding love. And let's face it; finding love again can be very, very challenging.

We have interviewed individuals over the years that confided in us that they doubted they could ever "strike another match" again when it came to finding new love.

We have met with many people who wanted new love so desperately. Most of these good people indicated to us that they did not want to grow old by themselves, but they admitted that finding love again wasn't easy. And, if you are one of those people who spent much of your life with someone you truly loved, finding new love again is especially complicated.

Truth is, good people are so desperate for love sometimes that they will forget their basic value system and look for love – any love – regardless of the consequence! Those that fall into this trap usually regret it.

Here's what we have found from our research over the years – finding love again is different than finding it the first time around. Make no mistake about that.

For example, the education level of your potential new partner is much more important the second time around. If you have a Ph.D. and you are dating a high school graduate, the chance of a lasting love is slim. Educational compatibility is far more important the second time around. Find someone whose education attainment is similar to yours.

Secondly, finding love again requires that you find someone who is secure within themselves – someone who likes living in their own skin.

Do they feel secure? Do they need external validation or are they content with their own validation? Falling in love again requires that you fall in love with someone who feels secure and self-confident. You cannot take the risk of falling in love all over again with someone who is insecure. Trust us on this. The research evidence is overwhelming.

Moreover, does your potential lover have a good self-concept? Do they feel good about themselves? Are they proud of themselves and their accomplishments? If they wallow in self-pity and self-doubt, they are probably not the one for you.

And here is a big one when it comes to finding love all over again. Are you falling in love with someone who has a sense of adventure when it comes to life? Are they content with the status quo or are they willing to "step outside the line" and be adventuresome, be daring, and live life to the fullest?

Sitting in a rocking chair is not the way to blissful life and love! Going to museums, zoos, concerts, and plays is fun and exhilarating. Hiking, biking, diving, gardening, dancing, walking and jogging are fun. If you desire these things, it stands to reason that you must find someone who values the same things as well.

And finally, does your new love interest like to read the newspaper, watch the news on television, keep informed about world events, and, in general, be an informed person? If they don't, perhaps you should find someone who does.

Our point in all this should be clear – if you want to find love the second time around you must look for someone who values and cherishes the things that matter the most to you. Don't fool yourself into thinking that you can find love the second time around with someone who is not like you.

When we are older and lose the one we love, we often find ourselves searching for true love again. Frankly, we must remember the most important lesson of all – finding true love again requires that we find someone we are compatible with, someone we are willing to share our life with, and someone who values what we believe to be important. To not recognize these things is to find yourself out of love again. Don't make that mistake.

Finding love again is never easy. Of that you can be sure. But one thing is for certain, you will not find true love again with someone whose likes and dislikes are not compatible with your own. It is not in the cards.

C H A P T E R 1 8

The Butterfly of Love

This love story has a most happy beginning.
Thank the butterfly.

ONE OF THE MOST TELLING questions in our interview protocol with people who say they have true love is this – "Can you imagine life without the one you love?" For those who truly love each other, the answer is always "NO!" Without fail, people who are deeply in love – deeply committed to each other – cannot imagine life without each other and when they share their answer, their eyes well up with tears as they contemplate the question – as they provide their "No" answer. Losing someone you love is experiencing your worst nightmare. Trust us on that.

But the truth is, some wonderfully loving relationships end because of the death of one of them. As hard as it is to imagine, sometimes the one you love dies. There is no way to sugarcoat this reality. When it happens it is devastating, it is awful, it is heartbreaking.

Recently, we heard a touching story from someone we met. Her story is one of those that inspires you. It is a story that tells you that finding true love all over again is possible – even after the death of a spouse.

Barb was awakened in the middle of the night and was told that her husband, who had been out of town on business, had been in an automobile accident involving a drunk driver. The policeman on the other end told her that her husband, Joe, was dead. Barb was stunned. She told the officer that he must be mistaken. Sadly, he was not. Joe was dead. She was now living her nightmare.

Over the weeks and months ahead it began to sink in to Barb that Joe was gone and that she would never see him again. Death is, as Barb found out, a permanent state.

For the next 11 years, Barb was content with an occasional date, but swore she would never again find such a wonderful and caring man like Joe. When he died, her perfect man was gone forever in her eyes and could never be replaced. She simply resigned herself to the fact that she would spend the rest of her life as a single, widowed woman. She had built a successful company in her hometown and devoted most of her energy to it. She was content with her life the way it was.

But a funny thing happened one day – a new man came into her life at the wonderful age of 57! His name was Tony, and Barb was smitten with him.

You see, Barb is a very attractive, highly confident, very feminine, assertive, self-sufficient, intelligent, well read, spiritual, and self-assured woman. She stays in great shape by walking, riding her bike, hiking, dancing, and playing tennis. For all these reasons, she was content to be single. And as you might guess, these same attributes scared away most men. It took a man with many of Barb's same characteristics to have the courage to ask her out on a date. Well, along came Tony. He asked her out and everything changed.

After their first date three months ago they have become virtually inseparable. They are always holding hands or in some way embracing each other as they visit the local zoo, the botanical garden, the art museum, or take in a concert together at the local symphony hall. More than anything, they love sharing meals together with a good bottle of wine, going fishing, learning how to dance the Tango, and cuddling on the couch as they talk endlessly into the night.

The other day Barb told us that she had found herself the man of her dreams. She was in love with a man who was similar in many ways to her deceased husband, Joe. And to her great satisfaction, her new beau, Tony, understands completely how much she loved her first husband and is not at all threatened by that. He loves her deeply and the feeling is certainly mutual.

Not so many months ago, Barb was sure she would never find another man to share her life with. She had told so many friends and acquaintances over the years that when Joe was killed, her "fire went out." But now she is fond of telling everyone, she "has struck another match!"

Falling in love again is somewhat like that elusive butterfly we have written about before. The butterfly of love can elude you until you sit quietly and patiently under a tall oak tree and contemplate the serenity and beauty of the moment – and then suddenly, the elusive butterfly of love will land on your shoulder.

Falling in love all over again can happen to you. It did to Barb. It did to Tony. This love story has a most happy beginning. Thank the butterfly.

HOW WILL I KNOW I AM IN LOVE?

SIMPLE THINGS MATTER

CHAPTER 19

How Will I Know I Am In Love?

You suddenly and out of
nowhere are inspired to say
I LOVE YOU! I LOVE YOU! I LOVE YOU!
You shout it to the stars. You are in love!

IN OUR MANY INTERVIEWS with people "in love" we ask them, perhaps, the most revealing question of the interview – "How will I know I am in love?" We have heard very consistent answers. And conversely, many people involved in a new loving relationship, particularly young people, often ask us, "How do I know if I am in love?" We think we know the answer.

While we have heard a number of answers to our "How do you know you are in love?" question, we can place them in ***seven*** categories. And, perhaps surprisingly, they have stayed the same over our 26 years of research on couples in love. Here they are, in a nutshell.

The first category is ***physical.*** People who say they are in love report getting "goosebumps," "a palpating heart," "sweaty palms," "a lump in my throat," "teary-eyed when I say goodbye," "a tingling sensation all over my body," and the like. People in love have a positive physical reaction when they think about or see the one they love in person.

The second category is ***emotional.*** When they think about or see the person they love, most lovers report similar feelings – "I laugh more often when I am with the person I love," "an uncontrollable smile comes over my face whenever I see her," and "I miss him when he leaves the room." People in love feel emotions for the person they love that they do not routinely feel for others.

The third category is ***positive worry.*** Over the years, we continue to be amazed about the consistency with which people in love report to us that they "worry about their lover" when they are not around. Little thoughts of what we have come to call "positive worry" about the one they love begins to creep into their mind – things like car accidents, falling down, getting hurt at work, and getting sick. The folks we interview for the most part do not worry compulsively or negatively. These thoughts are normal and natural when you are "in love."

The fourth category is what we call the ***I-cannot-imagine-life-without-her category.*** This is the point in love when you begin to think about the future – your future with the one you love. When you cannot imagine your life without him, you are in love!

The fifth category focuses on the ***oneness of your relationship.*** You begin to realize that you truly want this other person in your life. You want to be with them. You want to share with them. You want to live with them, share a bed with them, hold them and hug them. In our book, we refer to the notion of "turning two into one." You actually begin to think about the one you love and not just about yourself or your needs. You think about theirs – their wants, their needs, and their desires. When the feeling of oneness consumes your body you are in love!

The sixth category is about ***pre-occupied love.*** Simply stated, you think about the one you love most of the time. You can't get them out of your mind. You pull their photo out of your wallet and you smile. You are pre-occupied with them. When you are pre-occupied with them, you are in love with them!

The seventh and final category is ***love itself and your ability to express that love.*** You finally have the courage to tell them you love them! You miss them when they are not around. You worry about them. You care about their safety and welfare. You feel about them in ways you have never felt about another human being before. You suddenly and out of nowhere are inspired to say I LOVE YOU! I LOVE YOU! I LOVE YOU! You shout it to the stars. You are in love!

CHAPTER 20

What Does Love Look Like?

You can't fake love.
True love can be seen, felt,
observed, and heard.

WHILE WE HAVE WRITTEN about how you will know you are in love, about how you will feel when you are in love, about the importance of the human touch in expressing love, and about how love sounds, we haven't yet shared our observations and findings about what love ***looks like*** until today! So here goes.

When we interview successfully married couples we spend a lot of time observing them while we listen carefully to what they say. We record our observations. We make note of what we see. Oh, what they say is important, but what we see is even more so.

We have discovered that you can learn much about love from observing two people in love. So what does love look like? What do two people in love "say" through their interactions with the one they love? When you observe couples in love, how do they act? How do they interact? What do their actions tell you about their love for each other? Well, here's something to think about.

People in love can be observed:

Listening to each other intently; holding hands while they walk or sit; touching each other often; teasing each other in playful ways; smiling at each other; hugging each other; sharing a meal from the same plate; opening doors for each other; putting their arms around each other; talking to each other with full eye contact; sitting together touching each other; sharing the care of their children; picking up each other's plates and meal residue after eating at fast food restaurants; and walking next to each other.

The way people in love gaze at each other – the way they look lovingly at each other – tells you there is a "look of love."

These are just a few of the telltale signs of people in love. We bet you can name more, but the important point to remember is that it is hard to fake love. People, who observe people in love or those just pretending to be in love, know the difference! There is without a doubt "a look of love."

So, friends, our message about love being "an accumulation of the little things" should come through loud and clear again. You can't fake love. True love can be seen, felt, observed, and heard. Keep these simple things in mind next time you think about love.

We close with the words of Burt Bacharach in his very popular song, "The Look of Love."

I can hardly wait to hold you
Feel my arms around you
How long I have waited

Waited just to love you
Now that I have found you
Don't ever go.

There is no doubt – you can SEE love. You can't hide it. You can't fake it. You can't fool those who observe your relationship with each other.

To love is to show your love by your actions. To say you are in love doesn't count for much unless you show your love. To look like love is, more often than not, to be in love.

CHAPTER 21

Memories of Love at La Mediterranee

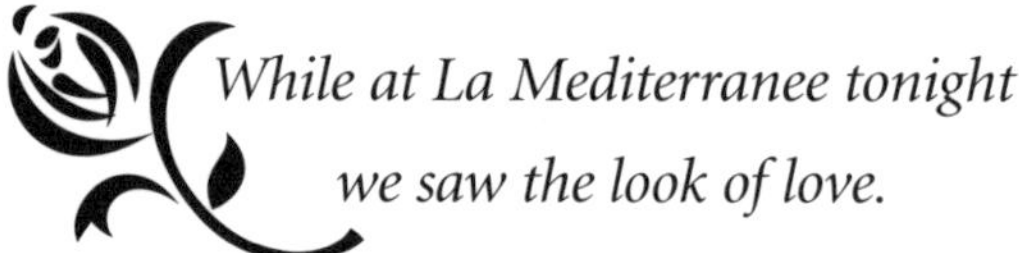

While at La Mediterranee tonight
we saw the look of love.

WE HAVE MANY MEMORIES of love. Tonight, we observed first-hand the look of love.

Nearly every time we go to New York City for business or pleasure, we go to a wonderful restaurant we discovered a number of years ago called ***La Mediterranee.*** This exquisite French bistro-style restaurant is located on 2nd Avenue just off 50th.

La Mediterranee reminds us so much of the intimacy you find in the bistros of France. And trust us on this; the quality of their food is as good as it gets! We have shared a romantic meal or two at many fine restaurants in Paris, Lyon, Nice, and at other gastronomically delightful restaurants in other French cities, but La Mediterranee ranks high on our list of destinations. If you want a great meal, a splendiferous bottle of French wine, and superb service in a warm and romantic environment, this is the place to be.

The décor of La Mediterranee has the look and feel of southern France. Paintings on the walls show scenes of France along the Mediterranean Sea, complete with beautiful beaches, blue skies, and charming and inviting scenes of French life.

We have found in our thousands of interviews with successfully married couples over the years that ***true love***, once found, is almost never lost. For many who have lost a spouse due to death, we have learned that true love lasts beyond a lifetime.

Memories of love found at our favorite New York City restaurant, La Mediterranee, are most certainly never lost. When you dine there, you never see anyone unhappy. You see couples of all ages enjoying the company of the one they love. You see budding romance.

When we left his restaurant tonight, Ernesto proudly proclaimed that at least two couples he had introduced to each other at his bar were now happily married! Which leads us to the main point of this article.

While at La Mediterranee tonight we saw the look of love. We saw the elderly man at the bar looking at the many loving couples in the restaurant as he quietly thought to himself how much he missed his own wife who had passed away. You could see in his eyes the love he had for his deceased wife and how much he wished she were back, sitting next to him sharing a drink. We felt for him. We felt his loneliness. We knew his life would probably never be the same without her.

Some couples sat at the bar. Most were young. They had their lives in front of them. They had their love in front of them.

Perhaps, Ernesto will introduce some of them to each other tonight. Ernesto has a good track record!

Most of the couples in La Mediterranee were like us – loving couples that had been married for many years – 42 for us. They, like us, were enjoying their love for each other over a magnificent meal on this beautiful evening in the Big Apple. Watching them gaze into each other's eyes made us proud – proud of their love and commitment to each other, proud of their willingness to let their love for each other show, proud of their adoration for the love of their life.

Next time you share a romantic meal with the one you love at La Mediterranee say hello to Ernesto, host and manager extraordinaire. He makes every dining experience a wonderful occasion. When you eat in Ernesto's restaurant, he makes you part of his family!

And don't forget to thank the best wait team there is – Pierre, Vito, Katja, and Mario – for their usual fabulous service. Ernesto is rightly proud of his colleagues. They make everyone's experience delightful and enjoyable.

Next time you are at La Mediterranee, ask Harold to play your favorite love song. He will mesmerize you with the way he strokes the ivory on his keyboard. If you want love songs, Harold's your inspiration. Hold her tight. Love him well! Harold will certainly help the romance.

Enjoy your memories of love from La Mediterranee. They will last a lifetime. Cherish them.

CHAPTER 22

In the Beginning Great Love Is Best Not Rushed

True and lasting love takes time
because true and lasting love
is all about the reciprocal gift of love
between two human beings.

A FEW DAYS AGO WE RAN across a marvelous quote by Jonathan Carroll, author of *Outside the Dog Museum.* It goes like this:

"You have to walk carefully in the beginning of love; the running across fields into your lover's arms can only come later when you're sure they won't laugh if you trip."

We think this is wonderful advice for those "falling in love." Too often, two people feel the early signs of a loving relationship only to move too fast and scare away the one they are falling in love with. Or worse yet, they become so enamored with "being in love" that they become blinded to the warning signs. They so desperately want to be in love and be loved that they miss important clues to the real feelings of the one they love.

In our many interviews over the years with individuals who have had a successful and long-term relationship with somebody, we have repeatedly heard this advice – go slow in the beginning.

You've heard the old expression, "Rome wasn't built in a day." One thing for certain – neither was love. It develops over time. It requires patience. It requires self-examination. And it most certainly requires you to run slowly across fields until you find the proper footing, lest you fall down!

Building confidence in any budding love relationship takes time and commitment. It requires a level of objectivity about what is going on at a level you may have never reached before. People falling in love do not lie to each other, but they often lie to themselves about what is happening to them. They let feelings and emotions get the best of them before they are truly ready to share their heart with another – before they are ready to make the honest and caring commitment required to make love last.

Recently, someone sent us a copy of a beautiful essay entitled *Letters To My Son* by Kent Nerburn. Our favorite passage is excerpted below:

Here "is where many lovers go wrong. Having been so long without love, they understand love only as a need. The first blush of new love is filled to overflowing, but as their love cools, they revert to seeing their love as a need. They cease to be someone who generates love and instead become someone who seeks love. They forget that the secret of love is that it is a gift, and that it can be made to grow only by giving it away."

The message here should be clear – love is a gift you give to someone, and if you are lucky, they give it back in return. But the real lesson here is that you need to step back and make sure that you feel good about giving your love away as a gift. And to do this takes time. It takes reflection. It requires being honest with yourself about what you are feeling and what you are giving away to another human being. Rushing to judgment about matters of such profound importance is never a wise thing to do. Giving love away takes time. Accepting true love takes courage. And trust. And time.

Recently, we wrote an article about love that captured the attention of many people around the world. We received an amazing amounts of comments about it. Bloggers picked it up. People talked about it. We entitled our article *How Will I Know I Am In Love?* We included it as the lead article in this section of the book because of its powerful message.

Our essential message in *How Will I Know I Am In Love?* is that there are clear and telltale signs for love. When you recognize those seven categories for knowing you are in love, honestly reflect upon them, and cherishing them as the gift of love that they are, you are in love. But don't confuse your feelings of love for another, your gift of love to another, without also truthfully asking yourself, "Have I also received the gift of love from the one I love?"

When you feel good about giving your love as a gift and that feeling is reciprocated by the one you love, then you both are in love with each other. As Nerburn tells us, the "secret of love is that it is a gift, and that it can be made to grow only by giving it away."

True and lasting love takes time because true and lasting love is all about the reciprocal gift of love between two human beings. To be in love is to dash across the field of lilies on a beautiful spring morning unafraid to fall down as you leap into the arms of the one you love and who loves you. Go, be in love if you are ready to give the gift of love.

CHAPTER 23

How Will I Know I Can Trust Him?

Words are cheap.
Actions mean everything!

HERE IS AN UNDENIABLE truth about life – actions speak louder than words! We know you've heard this all before! But the truth is you can, and must, judge a man by his actions and ***not*** by his words!

Words are cheap. Actions mean everything! The truth is always there for all to see when you observe the way people act and respond, rarely by what they say. This truth is self-evident – good men practice what they preach. Here's why.

In answer to the question, "How will I know I can trust him?" you must always remember this – you can tell a lot about a man by his actions. How does he respond to you? How does he treat you? How does he treat your friends, your family, your children, his dog, and all of the others you love? How does he treat the janitor? The person who cuts your grass? The checker at the supermarket?

Real men say what they mean and act the same way. Real men, good men, decent men, will always demonstrate who they are by their consistent actions. To know the real truth about a man – pay close and careful attention to him over a period of several weeks and then ask yourself this question – is he really what he appears to be? Consistent actions on his part will tell you what you need to know, for good or for bad.

Lately, we have been working with a couple who have been married for nearly 20 years and they are calling it quits. Why just today, she told us that it was time to get out of the relationship – time to "fish or cut bait." For nearly 20 years, her husband had mentally abused her and the children, while all the time boasting about how much he loved them. Actions speak louder than words!

The truth is, you can't really love your children when you constantly berate them. You can't truly love anyone that you put down, yell at, or constantly point out their failings and their frailties.

When you love someone, you learn to live with their failings, their mistakes, and their transgressions. In the end, you love them for what they are – for what they are in their heart and in their soul.

We all make mistakes. We all do dumb things from time to time. And the truth is, we more often than not, recover from the shortcomings we have. Honest, one-time mistakes are forgivable. On the other hand, repeated actions reveal who a person really is – for good or for bad.

A psychologist friend of ours reminds us from time to time about the "pervasive characteristics" present in human beings. These are "recurring patterns of thought and behavior" that defines a person – that tells us who they are. And recurring patterns of thought and behavior for the most part do not change when a person is an adult. In reality, these pervasive characteristics define who you are. Oh, sure, some people can cover up their real personality characteristics from time to time, but if you observe them long enough you will learn who they really are.

When someone you are observing over time repeatedly and consistently demonstrates through their actions and deeds the pervasive characteristics present in them, you must pay attention! If a man is truly a good person you can trust you will see it in their actions. Don't be fooled by words that are contrary to their actions.

All too often in life, people fall in love blindly. They refuse to make note of how the actions of another person define them. They pay too much attention to words and way too little to actions.

When you fall in love make it for all the right reasons. Don't ignore the signs. Don't ignore the glitches. Pay attention and your reward will, more often than not, be true love with a man you can trust. Ignore his actions and you do so at your own peril.

CHAPTER 24

When Am I Ready To Get Married?

Deciding if you are ready to get married begins with love. Agreement on the "core values" of marriage will grow the love, and doing the simple things day in and day out will sustain the love.

THIS MORNING WE HAD A delightful radio interview with a Pennsylvania radio station about our research on successful marriage. We have done a ton of these interviews since our book *Golden Anniversaries: The Seven Secrets of a Successful Marriage*, and we enjoyed them immensely.

It is always a pleasure to share the "secrets" of successful marriage with our interviewer and his or her audience. Sometimes we answer questions from the listeners, sometimes just from the host of the show, and at times from both. In this business, you learn pretty quickly to talk on your feet as the questions often come rapid-fire; many of them are questions you've never heard before; and the time to answer them is usually quite short.

Fortunately, over time we have developed the "gift of gab." And, because we know our subject quite well, based on our more than 26 years of research on successful marriage, most of our answers are easily retrievable from wherever it is stored in our respective brains!

This morning we got a question we have gotten before in some form or another, but not as directly or succinctly as the host asked it. His question – "When am I ready to get married?"

Over the years we have written about "How will I know I am in love?" We have waxed on about "the core values of successful marriage." And more often than we can remember, we have encouraged those in love to take our scientifically based marriage quiz to determine their "marriage compatibility." But the truth is, we have never directly addressed this important question. So today, we will do our best to share with you what we believe to be the answer to the question, "When am I ready to get married?"

First of all, the foundation of any successful marriage is ***love.*** Oh, sure, there are marriages of convenience, marriages based on religious or cultural customs (i.e., others determine who is married to whom), and marriages based on whim (think Las Vegas!). But the simple truth is most all successful marriages that stand the test of time, begin with love. So ingredient number one is, be in love. After reading the chapter entitled *How will I know I am in love?* you should be able to answer, "Yes we are truly in love."

The second ingredient is what we have come to call the "core values of successful marriage." Successfully married couples must share the same core values of love. Agreement on the core values is essential to building a healthy, happy, and long-lasting relationship. All too often, however, folks get married before they have honestly and truthfully determined the compatibility of their core value systems. Then guess what, they discover that all of the dreams and aspirations they have about their marriage aren't possible because the foundation of their relationship has cracks even before they start trying to build a life together. Core values matter and when they are incompatible, marriage should be reconsidered because later on, these differences will, more than likely, cause the marriage to crumble. Core values such as integrity, trustworthiness and unconditional love do matter.

Our advice is, two adults contemplating marriage should never delude themselves into thinking that their respective core value systems will change over time. They rarely do. Don't overlook the differences. Don't fool yourself into believing that you can "change him" or "change her." From what we know about personality development, adults are pretty much what they are. Many marriages that fail do so because the core values are not compatible. To think otherwise is to set yourself up for heartbreak further down the road of life.

The third ingredient associated with knowing if you are ready to get married or not is very, very simple. As we have said over and over in our many writings and interviews, simple things matter! Successful marriage is an accumulation of doing the simple things.

When you are contemplating marriage you should start to pay very close attention to the one you think you love. Do they do the simple things day in and day out, or not?

Here's a question to ask yourself, does he always get in line first at the fast-food restaurant to give his food order even though you, your parents, and others are in line with you? Does he open doors for you or does he go through the door first while he lets you fend for yourself? Does she want to tell you about her day but shows no interest in your day? You see, showing respect is a simple thing –

and it is easily observable. There is nothing complicated about it. If the one you purport to love is rarely respectful towards you, trust us on this – it will not get better with time. Observe the actions and deeds of the one you are thinking about marrying. Actions and deeds trump words every time!

Simple things matter, and the simple truth is if you do not see the behaviors you want and expect from the one you are thinking of marrying, it will only get worse over time.

Deciding if you are ready to get married begins with love. Agreement on the "core values" of marriage will grow the love, and doing the simple things day in and day out will sustain the love. These simple truths should be self-evident. Learn and understand these simple truths today so you too can celebrate your Golden Anniversary.

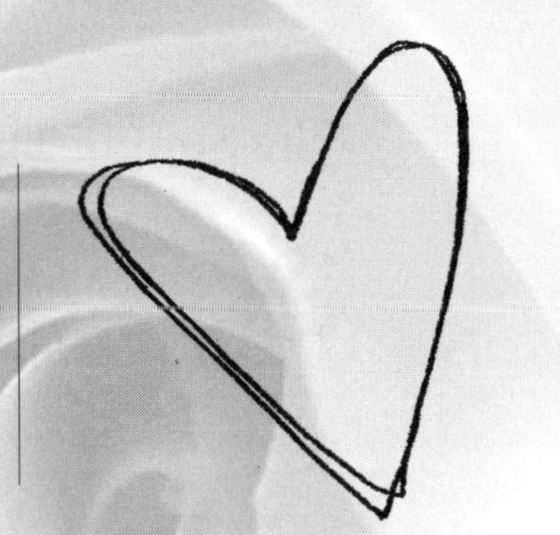

WHAT ARE THE SIMPLE THINGS THAT MATTERS?

SIMPLE THINGS MATTER

CHAPTER 25

The Simple Things That Matter

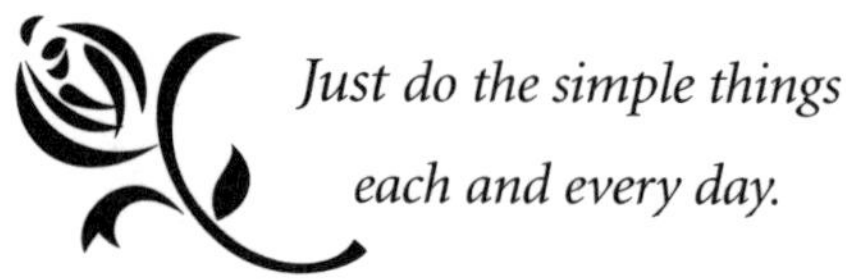

Just do the simple things each and every day.

IT IS AN ESTABLISHED FACT - successful love is based on an accumulation of the "simple things." We can state unequivocally, if you want your marriage or your relationship to succeed, you have to do the simple things each and every day.

To get you started right away, we put together a list of 50 examples of simple things that matter in love and marriage. This list is your first step in making your love survive and thrive over a lifetime together.

1. Take long walks together.
2. Snuggle in the morning before you get out of bed.
3. Recognize kindness with a thank you.

4. Call when you are going to be late.
5. Be generous with your time for each other.
6. Share a good bottle of wine while watching a sunset.
7. Compliment your lover about something he/she did today that made him/her special.
8. Hold hands often.
9. Bring home flowers for him/her when it is not a special occasion.
10. Leave a sticky note on your lover's wallet or purse telling him/her to come home safely to you because you love him/her.
11. Ask your spouse about their dreams and desires for your future together.
12. Open doors for each other.
13. Bike ride together, bringing a picnic lunch for a secluded spot along the way.
14. Walk your dog together while discussing the issues of the day.
15. Fix your lover breakfast in bed for no special reason.
16. Say "I love you" several times during each day.
17. Treat your lover with courtesy at all times.
18. Help clean off the table and do the dishes after dinner.
19. Compliment your lover's cooking.
20. Tell him/her one reason why he/she means so much to you.
21. Take your spouse to their favorite restaurant in the middle of the week.
22. Touch your mate 100 times a day.
23. Surprise your spouse by bringing lunch when least expected.
24. Prepare meals together as often as you can.
25. Spend an evening listening to music and making a CD of your favorite songs together.
26. Upend expectancies and delight your lover. Make things exciting.

27. Always point out the positive attributes of your lover, both at home and in public.
28. Give your husband or wife a massage or a back rub.
29. Look directly into your lover's eye when you are having a conversation.
30. Be your lover's best cheerleader for their accomplishments.
31. Plan a bubble bath together and see where it leads.
32. Go dancing together.
33. Talk about everything. No topic is too small or too big. There are no sacred cows.
34. Always demonstrate respect for each other in your words and in your actions.
35. Schedule your annual physicals on the same day.
36. Plan a week of healthy meals together with foods that you both enjoy.
37. Write your husband/wife a love letter and leave it for him/her to find in their underwear drawer.
38. Sit down and go over the finances together before you pay the bills for the month.
39. Take your lover to a movie, putting your arm around them like you used do when you were dating.
40. Go for a boat ride, car ride or train ride that isn't planned and doesn't have an itinerary.
41. Write personal Valentine's Day cards.
42. Turn off the television and talk to each other.
43. Sing a song together and to each other.
44. Go to Disneyland—just the two of you.
45. Plant flowers together.
46. Share a tuna melt.
47. Kiss each other passionately.
48. Go to the zoo together.
49. Share a shower
50. Sit in your porch swing and gaze at the stars.

You see, the simple things do matter. Change your relationship and your life in positive ways by doing the simple things. Start today.

While these 50 ideas are good examples of the simple things that can get you started, the remaining chapters of this book are filled with powerful ideas about simple things that can sustain your love for a lifetime.

CHAPTER 26

Love IS Having to Say Your're Sorry

This simple notion may very well be one of the great truths about loving, successful, and long-lasting relationships.

THE MOST FAMOUS LINE FROM the wildly popular 1970 book (and subsequent movie), *Love Story,* by Erich Segal is, "Love means never having to say you are sorry." As a *New York Times* number one bestseller, the book became the top selling work of fiction for all of 1970 in the United States, and was translated into more than 20 languages worldwide according to Wikipedia. The motion picture of the same name was the number one box office attraction of 1971."

The opening narrative of the book by the main character, Oliver, says, "What can you say about a twenty-five-year-old girl who died? That she was beautiful and brilliant? That she loved Mozart and

Bach, the Beatles, and me?" The rest of the book is just as riveting, trust us on that.

Love Story is a beautiful story. If you have any heart at all, you will cry your eyes out after reading the book or watching the movie. In the end, Jenny dies and we are all heart-broken. Lessons abound.

Segal's work is a true romantic story about love, life, and death. It touched the hearts of everyone who read the book or saw the movie. The problem is, the basic premise of the most famous line of the book is "Love is never having to say you are sorry, is wrong. Love IS having to say you are sorry!

Love Story is a book about one of the great love stories of the 20th Century. There are many lessons about love and life. But the most famous lesson of the book is a lesson you should not learn, and we wonder from time to time if many of the failed marriages over these past 37 years in the United States and around the world might in some way be related to the notion that being in love does not require you to apologize when you do or say something wrong.

What is so confusing about the message of the book and the movie is this – because we are in love with someone, does that make us immune from apologizing for our bad behavior? Just because we are married or engaged to someone, are we exempt from saying **I'm sorry** when we hurt our lover's feelings or disappoint them with our words and actions.

From time to time in any loving relationship, things can go awry. People who love each other get angry. They yell at each other and say hurtful things. We all make mistakes in judgment. Sometimes we show our dark side to the people we love. And frankly, there are times when we make fools out of ourselves around the ones we love.

When two people love each other, they feel more comfortable discussing perplexing or challenging problems. They are willing to address the tough issues head on. Why, because they trust each other more than they trust any other human being. They feel comfortable with the one they love. And because their comfort level is so high they often say and do things to each other that are hurtful. But because they love each other and trust each other, does it give them carte-blanche license to say and do whatever they want, even if it is damaging or hurtful? Of course not! But the reality is that it happens and the wounds can be deep. Feelings can be hurt. Relationships strained.

Which leads us to the most important point of this chapter – love IS having to say you are sorry. There are no ifs, ands, or buts about it. When you engage in behavior, actions, or words that are hurtful and damaging in your relationship with the one you love, you not only should apologize, you MUST do so! In our humble opinion, no two people who profess to love each other can ever take the position that they don't have to apologize to each other for saying and doing hurtful things. And, never take the position that "Oh, they know I love them. I don't have to say I'm sorry." The latter is one of the most egregious of all sins you can commit in your relationship with the one you love – taking them for granted.

In the end, there is only one correct action to take when you hurt the one you love. You must say you are sorry. Contrary to what Jenny said to Oliver in *Love Story,* LOVE IS HAVING TO SAY YOU ARE SORRY. This simple notion may very well be one of the great truths about loving, successful, and long-lasting relationships – one of the great truths about marriages and relationships that celebrate their golden anniversaries.

CHAPTER 27

Toilet Seat Love

Toilet Seat Love describes just one of those simple things that really matter.

AS WE SAY REPEATEDLY, the simple things matter in love and marriage. Do the simple things and your marriage or loving relationship will prosper.

Charley learned his lesson some 40 years ago! He grew up in a rural area of Missouri back when outhouses were more prevalent than toilets that flushed! When we first got married some 42 years ago, Charley, "the consummate gentleman" as Liz refers to him, had to learn an important lesson about toilet seats.

As it turns out, toilet seats are designed to protect women and save marriages! There are four kinds of husbands when it comes to *Toilet Seat Love.* Here they are, briefly described.

First, husband number one goes to the bathroom. He lifts the seat and goes, then replaces the seat in its down position. Wife loves husband when he does this! The marriage is saved!

Husband number two fails to lift the seat and, thusly, goes ON the seat. But, being a kind and respectful husband, he cleans up his mess with a handful of Kleenex. Wife still loves husband but not as much.

The third kind of husband goes to the bathroom, doesn't lift the seat, goes ON seat, doesn't clean seat, and wife sits in his mess later that day. Wife is not happy with husband! Trust us on this.

The fourth kind of husband raises the seat before he goes, but leaves seat in the upright position when he is done. Later that day, wife sits in the toilet bowl and the impact splashes toilet bowl contents on the floor. Occasionally, she gets stuck in bowl and needs assistance in getting out. Wife does not love husband when he does this. The marriage is in jeopardy!

We hope you enjoyed the levity of this little story but, more importantly, you find its meaning to be helpful as you think about the little things that make your loving relationship with someone else thrive. *Toilet Seat Love* describes just one of those simple things that really matter. Always remember that lasting relationships and successful marriages are built on an accumulation of the simple things.

CHAPTER 28

iPod Love

The time you spend together is precious. Walking and talking is one of the best things couples can do for their relationship.

WHEN THE IPOD CAME on the market several years ago, we were one of the first "kids" on the block to own one. Since we have been Mac users since the 80's, buying one of these babies was a natural thing for us to do. And since both of us love music and both have very eclectic music tastes, the thought of downloading a billion songs gave us chills up and down our respective spines! To date, we have about 9000 songs on our iPods. Not quite a billion but we are working on it!

Now, you are asking yourself, what does the iPod have to do with love and marriage? Well, it goes like this. Remember our constant refrain regarding successful loving relationships – "Love is simple to understand. The problem is people won't do the simple things required to make love work." The iPod is a good example.

We walk a lot and we always take our Wonder Dog, Jake, with us. The many miles we spend walking around our lovely hometown of St. Louis has allowed us to solve most of the problems in the universe! If we could walk more there would be world peace, everybody would have a job, there would be no empty stomachs, and everybody would love each other. Talking and walking is fun and probably has as much to do with our own successful 42-year marriage as anything we do. And our creativity begins to explode on those walks. Everything seems possible. Every problem seems solvable.

Here is where the iPod comes in.

When we first got our iPods we started listening to them as we walked. Oh, sure, the exercise was still good and the music was beautiful. The fresh air still smelled the same. But guess what happened – we stopped talking when we walked. It didn't take long for us to realize how much we were missing on our walks. Our creativity began to wane, and for the first time in many years, we began to feel a little tension in our relationship.

Since both of us have worked for a combined 90+ years, we needed those walks together to problem solve and to do the creative thinking required for our books, our research, and our other writings. Those walks were important quality time together. They were so important to our mental health as well. Now, we were messing up all the good things because we were listening to our iPods when we were together instead of to each other.

We also began to notice other couples (lovers, friends) wearing their iPods as they walked with each other. And they weren't talking, just like we weren't! Something had to be done and we did it – no more walking with each other while listening to our iPods. No more sitting together in the family room listening to our iPods. No more listening to our iPods when were together except when we were on a plane flying somewhere. Since the normal noise on a plane makes it hard to talk anyway, the iPod shuts out the bad noise and replaces it with beautiful music.

Don't get us wrong – we love our iPods. We can't imagine being without them. But like most things in life, there is a time and place for everything. The time you spend together is precious. Walking and talking is one of the best things couples can do for their relationship. Leave the iPod at home when you share those moments. Save the iPod for the times you are alone or on a noisy plane. Your relationship and your love will thank you for it.

Those Golden Anniversaries we write about are often achieved as a result of lots of walking and talking! Maybe we will see you on one of those walks. Without the iPods of course!

WHAT MAKES LOVE LAST?

SIMPLE THINGS MATTER

CHAPTER 29

The Foundation of Love Is Trust

Being honest and trustworthy
is at the heart of all the best
loving relationships we have studied.

SUCCESSFULLY MARRIED COUPLES never cheat on their spouse! To be truly in love is to be unequivocally and unconditionally dedicated to the one you love. To betray your spouse in intimate ways is to destroy your relationship, make no mistake about that. Most marriages cannot recover from this form of betrayal. Don't fool yourself into thinking it can.

Over the past 26 years when conducting our interviews with successfully married couples we are always profoundly struck by their undying trust in each other. They literally trust each other with their lives, their well-being, and their sacred honor. The words they use to describe the one they love, more often than not, include words and expressions like trust, honesty, loyalty, respects me, admires me, always there for me, never lets me down, truthful, and never lies to me. Their trust for each other is about as complete as you can get. And when we ask couples in love during our interviews to place, in an overall sense, where their relationship is on a 10-point scale with 10 being "Absolute Trust," without exception, they say "10!" Isn't that wonderful? Remarkable? These are the couples that will celebrate their golden anniversaries together!

Trust is not something all loving relationships start with. For some couples the trust becomes complete in a few years. For others, it takes awhile. But one thing is for sure, happy and successful marriages and relationships survive and thrive on the basis of this trust. Trust is so pervasive in their relationship that they never give it a second thought. They expect it. It's always there. It is part of the fabric of their relationship.

There is one thing you can take to the bank – all people in love have faced temptations in their relationship. The pretty girl in the restaurant captures your fancy. The handsome man walking down the street draws your attention. The flirt at work is tempting at times. And, we will dare say, sometimes in every relationship you think about slipping in the sack with some of the beautiful people you meet. But here's where it stops – these are only fleeting moments of passing fancy. These are the moments of momentary lust for another human being that are not acted on.

Why? People in love who are happy in their relationships control their urges because they know that while a moment of sexual fantasy is healthy and normal, following through and enjoying sexual satisfaction with someone other than their mate – cheating on their mate – is destructive to the loving and trusting relationship between them. It's okay to have sexual urges and fantasies regarding another person, but to act on them ruins all that trust. It destroys the tie that binds.

Couples who are truly in love in their relationship know that a few moments of sexual satisfaction can NEVER replace the loving, trusting, and caring relationship they have developed with their mate. As someone once said to us, "I have a marriage license but I didn't give up my looking license!" Admiring others in intimate ways is normal and healthy. But acting on those urges has ruined many a marriage and many a loving relationship.

Those wonderful couples we have interviewed resist these normal urges and temptations of life because they know their relationship is so much more important to them. Destroying the trust between them causes the foundation of their relationship to crumble.

Character in a successful marriage or relationship does matter, and character is about trust. Being honest and trustworthy is at the heart of all the best loving relationships we have studied. It really is a 10 on a 10-point scale. In our estimation, character is the foundation of true love!

The foundation of true love is trust. Destroy that foundation and you destroy your love. When you do so there is rarely redemption – there is rarely ever reconciliation. Never forget this simple truth – there is character in the best loving relationships. Practice good character and your love will not only survive, it will thrive.

CHAPTER 30

Compatibility: The Core Values of Love

The Core Values of all successful loving relationships are at the heart of the matter.

WE HAVE LEARNED A LOT about successful love and marriage in the USA and around the world over these past 26 years of research. What we would like to do in this chapter is share with you what we have found to be the Seven Core Values of All Loving Relationships.

Over the past 26 years, we have learned much about what makes great marriages tick - about what makes them successful. Even in spite of ominous odds from time to time, the best marriages survive and thrive, and we know why! They survive and thrive because they are committed to the Core Values present in all great marriages and successful loving relationships. Here they are in a nutshell.

1. The couple in love is committed to always putting each other first in their relationship with each other.

The first thing you notice in all highly successful loving relationships is that those who purport to be in love recognize that their relationship is not about you and me, it is about US. Discovering that YOU are not the center of the universe is the hallmark of a great relationship. Actually putting another human being number one is a powerful indication that you are truly in love.

2. The couple in love is committed to democracy in their relationship.

Always remember, successful loving relationships are egalitarian. Namely, the best relationships understand that theirs is a shared relationship. If one person has all the power and makes all the decisions, it is NOT love! True love is a very democratic thing!

3. The couple in love is committed to ensuring their mutual happiness.

Remember, true love is not just about ensuring your happiness. More importantly, and often for the first time in your life, you actually enjoy and are motivated by ensuring the happiness of someone other than yourself. It is a good feeling!

4. The couple in love values absolute trustworthiness and integrity in their relationship with each other.

If you cannot trust the one you love, then it is not true love! Trust us on that. The most successful loving relationships report that they trust their mate unequivocally and without hesitation. To violate that trust is to undermine and, ultimately destroy, the relationship with the one you say you love.

5. The couple in love is committed to caring and unconditional love for each other.

When you truly love someone you do so without conditions. It is not about loving you IF . . . True love is unconditional.

6. The couple in love is committed to being mutually respectful towards each other.

There is a Golden Rule in true love and it is like the one you learned early in your life – "Do unto others as you would have them do unto you." Do not expect to be treated with respect when you are disrespectful to the one you love. Respectfulness is at the heart of all great loving relationships.

7. The couple in love values their mutual sense of responsibility for each other.

People in love care for each other in ways that they have never cared for another human being. They feel a sense of responsibility for another person that they have never felt before. It feels so good to put another's needs above your own. To do so is to love deeply.

The *Core Values* of all successful loving relationships are at the heart of the matter. If you and your mate master these values, your love will, in all probability, last a lifetime.

CHAPTER 31

For Love and Tuna Melts

Quite frankly, every person we know needs a place that takes them in, surrounds them with warmth and love, and lets them be what they aspire to be.

EVERYBODY NEEDS A PLACE to call home! Everybody needs a place to call home that is away from home. Quite frankly, every person we know needs a place that takes them in, surrounds them with warmth and love, and lets them be what they aspire to be. Everybody needs a place that unleashes their creative energies.

Nearly every Saturday or Sunday for several years we have gone to a favorite restaurant of ours in St. Louis to talk about our research, about love and marriage, and about all of the wonderful couples we have interviewed. Many of our best ideas about our book have been given birth at *Fuzio.* In fact, we could argue that our book was birthed at *Fuzio!*

Truth is, we love *Fuzio!* They have great people who work for them, terrific ownership, a wonderful environment, and great food. And while we go there for all this, we go primarily because some of our best thinking about our work occurs there. *Fuzio* is a supportive place where everybody knows your name – where your waiter and your host actually care about you as a person – where the food actually lives up to its hype. What cool people work at Fuzio! We love them!

We certainly love their food. Frankly, we think it energizes us. In fact, their food may actually possess some secret ingredients that stimulate us on to better thinking and to better writing. We think it is the Tuna Melt with Field Greens or Greek Salad that makes us clear thinkers. Sometimes, Liz will swear that it's the Pad Thai that makes all good things happen. Charley swears by the Tuna Melt. In her quiet moments, Liz agrees – it's the Tuna Melt! Well, the Pinot Grigio helps as well! And the company.

Whether it's the Tuna Melt, the Pinot Grigio, or the Pad Thai, one thing is clear about *Fuzio* and places like it – everybody needs a place where they can go to unwind and think freely and creatively about things that matter in life, love, and in their work. For us, it is *Fuzio.* And because of all this, we owe them a lot. We attribute much of our creative energy to them.

We have studied successful love, marriage, and relationships around the world. We have eaten many different and exciting foods, sampled a variety of wines, stayed in interesting places, and met extraordinary people. But through it all, we always come back to the importance of being around honest and loving people. Our life's work has not occurred in isolation from good, decent, and caring people. And yours has not either. In love and in life, people need people. It is hard to imagine life without honest, hard-working, trustworthy, and supportive people around us at every turn. Life and love do not exist in a vacuum.

So, friends, may you have your *Fuzio* as we do – a place where you go to meet good people within a supportive environment. A place where your creative energies burst forth with unique and clever ideas. A place where your best thinking occurs. And above all, a place that will take you in when there is no other place to go with your best ideas. *Fuzio* is that place for us.

So tonight, we want to thank the *Fuzio* manager, Terese, and the marvelous folks who have served us the great food that inspires us – Myriah, Beeb, Stacie, Jo, and Grace Marie. They help make our life joyful. They help make our life rich. Good people like these are the ones who make you want to write about love, friends, and relationships.

Love and a Tuna Melt – they go together like wine and cheese. They go together like a good book and a warm fireplace. They go together like us and *Fuzio.*

Go find your *Fuzio!*

CHAPTER 32

The Loving Touch

It is their way of saying
"I love you so much
I simply must touch you."

WE BEEN MARRIED FOR 42 years and simply can't keep our hands off of each other! For many years, we thought we were unique. Then we started our research for our book, and did we get a big surprise – virtually every happily married couple we interviewed reported the same condition! Over time we have come to call it the "tactile response." Literally translated, it means, "I touch you here, I touch you there, I touch you everywhere!"

During our interviews with married couples we pay a lot of attention to their tactile interactions. More often than not, they sit on the couch during the interview and hold hands or place some part of their body on their mate's body. It is their way of saying "I love you so much I simply must touch you." So why all of this touching?

As part of our interviews we asked the couples to tell us what they believe to be the most endearing and important characteristics of their spouse. We continued with the following questions: "How would you describe your spouse? What adjectives would you use?" Here are the words we most often heard: encouraging, positive, loving, honest, has integrity, beautiful (or handsome), understanding, wonderful, patient, loves life, loves me, unselfish, giving, caring, trusting, generous, helpful, conscientious, and humorous. Words to live by in a marriage, wouldn't you say? And they said these things unabashedly, without apologies.

Successful couples know nearly everything about each other. They have studied in infinite detail how their spouse looks, feels and acts. They know what makes the one they love tick and can recite in scripture and verse their best qualities. They brag about each other all the time. They love each other for a whole bunch of reasons and don't mind telling you what they are.

What do their words about each other have to do with touching? Here's what we observed during our many interviews – when couples told us something special about their spouse in response to our questions, they would touch each other as if to emphasize the importance of the words. Touching was like an exclamation mark! Over time, we believe that these couples, like the two of us, say these words with a touch, without always saying the words out loud. Touching becomes kind of a ***Morse Code*** – a substitute for language and the expression of feeling. Successfully married couples have mastered the ***Morse Code*** of marriage – it's called touching.

A wise person once said that if you pass your spouse 100 times a day, you should touch them 100 times a day. When you touch someone, you are acknowledging his or her presence and expressing your love. In effect you are saying, "I love you so much I simply must touch you.

CHAPTER 33

What's Sex Got to Do with It?

If you think anybody's marriage is going to last 30 or more years just because they have good sex – well, forget it! It isn't going to happen.

OLDER ADULTS BETWEEN THE ages of 57 and 85 make sex an important part of their lives! That's the results of the first comprehensive national survey of the sexual attitudes and behaviors of older adults as reported in the *New England Journal of Medicine.* And, as you might have guessed, our 26 years of research with successfully married couples found the same conclusions.

For sure, every happily married couple we have interviewed reported at least a reasonable degree of satisfaction with their sex life. But you know what, NOT ONE of the couples we interviewed who had been married 30-77 years reported that their sex life was central to overall success of their relationship. Not one! Sure it was important, but if you think anybody's marriage is going to last 30 or more years just because they have good sex – well, forget it! It isn't going to happen.

Lasting marriages are characterized by frequent moments of intimacy and bliss. Over the years, we have had a wonderfully healthy sexual relationship with each other. Sometimes our sex is so good . . . . . well, we won't bore you with the details!

We could wax on and on about the role of sex in a marriage, but others have done that over and over. Those who write about sex all the time might have contributed to much of the dysfunctionality surrounding sex in relationships. Frankly, some popular books we have seen on the subject hold up a standard of sexual performance and gratification that hardly any couple could achieve. And worse yet, couples that can't live up to the "standard" think they've failed. Many times their relationship suffers.

Our message should be clear to our readers – in successful marriages sex can be fun, important, and a healthy way of being intimate with your partner. Just because you get older and have been married for 30 years or more does not mean that your sexual life has to be less active. On the other hand, based on our research and first-hand experience, we think it is grossly overemphasized in terms of its centrality to successful and long-term marriages. So much more is present in those relationships that pass the test of time. Sex is only one of them and is certainly not the most important for couples with long lasting successful marriages.

As the study in the *New England Journal of Medicine* points out, the sexual activity of older adults is not as much tied to their age as it is to their physical health. In the next chapter called ***Physical Love*** we talk about how successfully married couples focus on each other's physical health. So, even though sex is not central to the overall success of your marriage, we would like to leave you with this final thought – if you would like to continue enjoying sex into your later years, take time today to focus on the physical health of both you and the one you love.

C H A P T E R 3 4

Physical Love

Frankly, and in our humble opinion,
we have a mutual responsibility
to each other to do our best to
maintain our health.

OW THAT WE HAVE YOUR ATTENTION . . .

We completed our annual physical examinations today. Long ago we established the tradition of scheduling our respective annual physicals on the same day. Why, you ask? It's simple really – we love each other from the bottom of our respective hearts and want to be around each other for as much as we can for as long as we can.

Think about it – beyond your own health whose health do you concern yourself with the most? We bet it is the one you love the most. In the loving relationships we have observed over the years, including our own, we note how much happier people are in their lives when they are personally healthy and when the one they love the most is healthy as well.

Frankly, and in our humble opinion, we have a mutual responsibility to each other to do our best to maintain our health. We eat well, take our vitamins, are religious about taking our medications every day, and riding our bikes on the many trails in St. Louis has become nearly addictive. We encourage each other to do all of these things and then top off our year by having our annual physicals. It is always better to catch a health problem in the very early stages so a physical exam is a must. Oh, and the good news is – we passed our physicals with flying colors!

Doing our best to stay healthy for ourselves and for the ones we love is the best way we can think of to say, “I love you.” And being healthy makes that “physical love” all the more fun and exciting!

Here’s to your health!

CHAPTER 35

Never Go to Bed Mad at Each Other

Do not be fooled by those who tell you that it is not important to resolve divisive issues before you go to bed.

On the *Today Show* a remarkable segment aired. It was remarkable not because it was good or enlightening, but because it wasn't. In fact, it was downright misleading and irresponsible based upon the research evidence, and we want to comment on it.

A psychologist and the managing editor of *Good Housekeeping* were on the *Today Show* to proclaim that the notion of "never go to bed mad at each other" was a myth. Imagine, calling such a time-honored notion a myth. Listening to them made our skin crawl and here's why – credible research does not support what they said.

We have learned a lot about what makes good marriages work interviewing thousands of successfully married couples. Towards the end of our interview protocol we ask these wonderful couples if they could offer three pieces of advice that we could share with newlyweds. And guess what, the number one piece of advice they have given, and it is has been consistent over the years, is "Never go to bed mad at each other!"

Remember, this advice comes from happily married couples. The advice they give isn't designed to shock the media with something unusual or out of the ordinary. These are the words of couples with a proven track record. Frankly, we got the impression when we watched the *Today Show* that the purpose of referring to "Never go to bed mad at each other" as a myth was to get a spot on a highly watched morning television show! But the sad truth is, their message was a terrible message to send to newly married couples. Our fear – they just might listen to the advice they heard on TV and that would be a big mistake in our judgment.

From time to time you hear so-called experts throw out information as if it were scientific fact. People believe it as if it were gospel. The problem is, much of what you hear has no scientific or research base.

The good news about the notion of "Never go to bed mad at each other" – it is based on research from those who would know best – those who have been happily, blissfully, and successfully married for 30-77 years! The lessons learned from ***15,000 years of successful marriage*** speak for themselves.

Married couples do, from time to time, have disagreements. They argue over big things and little things. They argue over stuff that doesn't matter and stuff that does. But here is what we have learned from our research – successfully married couples rarely ever go to bed without resolving their differences on an issue, be it big or small. Many report to us that they have stayed up all night trying to bring closure to an issue that has divided them. They know that gaining resolution is far more important than getting a good night's sleep. And remember this, issues that are not attended to more often than not fester through the night and only appear worse in the morning.

Do not be fooled by those who tell you that it is not important to resolve divisive issues before you go to bed. They are simply misguided and the advice they give can be hurtful to your relationship. Accept the advice of those who know – those whose marriages are happy and have stood the test of time.

CHAPTER 36

Enhance Your Love With Privacy

The recognition and practice of the absolute need for privacy and aloneness is, in our judgment after analyzing thousands of interviews, a fundamental predisposition of successful marriages.

WE HAVE WITNESSED time and time again marriages in which one or both partners failed to understand the importance of being alone, not only for themselves, but for their spouse as well. When we first introduce this concept to others, the reaction is usually one of surprise. Many couples are of the mistaken notion that they are to be constantly attentive to their spouse. While their intentions are good, their desire to be attentive causes them to, in fact, interfere with the quality of their communicative relationship with their mate. The desire for too much closeness can inadvertently drive a wedge between husband and wife. Isn't that ironic?

In all probability, many couples believe that quantity of time together is the most important characteristic of their relationship. Instead, the "law of diminishing returns" comes into play here. The economists would explain it something like this. Let's say you buy a case of your favorite cola and decide to drink it in one setting. The first cola tastes great. Perhaps the first two or three taste good. But after about four or five, the quality of taste begins to diminish. If you were to drink the whole case in one setting, you would like each cola less and less until you reached a point where you began to absolutely hate your favorite cola. The "law of diminishing returns" seems to appropriately describe many marriages doesn't it? More is not always better. Give your spouse some privacy . . . the opportunity to be alone. Expect the same opportunity for yourself. Don't allow communication in your marriage to fall victim to the "law of diminishing returns."

In our interviews, we have been continuously reminded of the importance of privacy and aloneness to the success of a marriage. The recognition and practice of the absolute need for privacy and aloneness is, in our judgment after analyzing thousands of interviews, a fundamental predisposition of successful marriages. The amount of time available to satisfy these two needs varies from one marriage to another and from one marriage partner to another. But one thing is clear, all marriages will stand the test of time only if these duel needs are recognized and respected. How do you and your spouse improve the quality of communication based on this notion?

Each individual has a different level of need that can change at different stages in their life. Understanding and recognizing the level of need can be quite difficult at times, especially for a person with a low level of need for privacy and aloneness. Being alone to your thoughts provides for you a periodic psychological renewal. A few moments alone to your thoughts each day frees the spirit and cleanses the soul. Do not deny yourself these moments together with yourself. You know what we are talking about don't you? Remember, to recognize that your spouse also has these same needs.

Just as important is assuring yourself and your spouse that it is natural to have this need and that everyone has this need. In other words, feeling guilty about needing and wanting alone time is not appropriate or healthy. Recognize the need and embrace it.

If you and your spouse allow each other time for privacy and aloneness, think of the possibilities. The quality of communication can only be enhanced between the two of you after refreshing your mind and spirit with alone time. Did you ever notice how hard it is to talk and listen to someone else when your mind is overflowing with thoughts about work, home, children, and the like? No matter how hard you try, you listen but you do not really hear. And you want to know why? It is because you have denied yourself those moments of belonging only to yourself. What kind of real communication goes on between the two people in a marriage within this context? We believe the evidence is clear – not much!

Isn't it interesting that at the root of successful communication with your mate is no communication at all? You'll have to admit, this is an interesting notion with considerable merit. While we were quite taken with the idea in our early interviews with successful couples, it was not until some of their stories and examples so poignantly illustrated the concept that we fully grasped the importance of the need for privacy and aloneness to respect. Sometimes we try so hard to be great communicators that we end up with results opposite of our intentions. Because of our social nature, we have been misled into believing that we must always socialize. You only have to consider this for a moment to see the fallacy in this kind of thinking.

If we were pressed, we would probably admit that privacy and aloneness have been at the top of our list of needs many times in our marriage. We live such hectic lives at work that the time to be alone with our own thoughts is paramount to our engaging in any meaningful communication with each other. The recognition and respect for these dual needs are fundamental to successful communication in a marriage. If we are unable to communicate, nothing else matters.

You have to belong to yourself before you can belong to others. Do not miss the opportunity. As the song goes "Even lovers need a holiday . . . time away . . . from each other!"

CHAPTER 37

Lasting Love

There is much to learn from these two lovebirds who have found "Lasting Love."

LASTING LOVE, 'til death do us part. Married couples repeat this stanza or some variation of it in most marriage ceremonies. In its essence, two people commit to each other their love, their faithfulness, and their sacred honor for the rest of their lives. Many times, it works out just that way. Other times, the promise falls short. But in the case of Sandy and Pris, love is alive and well and will be sustained for a lifetime.

Of all the interviews we have conducted throughout the USA and around the world, no love seemed greater than the love between Sandy and Pris. These two are a perfect example of what it means to find lasting love.

We interviewed them in their home about two and a half years ago. Sandy has retired as CEO of a large American corporation. He is now investing his time and money in philanthropic causes across the USA, particularly in character education. Pris has always been interested in the arts and is a big supporter of opera theatre, in particular. Their passion for their philanthropic causes was amazing and their commitment to their work was heartwarming. If you ever wanted to spend an evening with two of the most generous, endearing, enchanting, and wonderful people you could meet, these are the two that you would want to be with.

Before we interviewed Sandy and Pris, we thought we knew a lot about love and relationships. That evening, however, we got an education for which we will be eternally grateful.

Sandy loves Pris absolutely and completely. He loves her without conditions. He has loved her since the first time he saw her on the ski slopes near Santa Fe, New Mexico. During our interview, he looked at his bride of nearly 60 years and said, "She is still the same beautiful woman I married 60 years ago!" He had tears in his eyes. Pris choked back the tears, as she looked deep into his eyes. These were the faces of love.

Pris responded that she fell in love with this handsome, dashing man with his white skis as soon as she saw him glide effortlessly down the snow-covered mountain.

Sandy and Pris love each other from the bottom of their respective hearts and both say this today, "We have been married for more than 60 years and are more in love now than ever." Everything they said to us during the interview reinforced their unqualified love for each other.

There are many lessons to be learned from Sandy and Pris. We want to share with you what they believe to be the most important.

First, they share a mutual admiration society. They always support and encourage each other.

Secondly, they love each other very much and say so many times during each day of their lives.

Thirdly, they are totally honest with each other. They show integrity in their interactions, have undying trust in each other, and demonstrate their character by their words and by their actions.

And finally, their most important lesson of all – "Never go to bed mad at each other."

Sandy and Pris have great admiration and respect for each other. It shows in their words, their actions, their expressions, and in Sandy's case, in his voice as he sings love songs to her every morning – off key sometimes, but always full of love and emotion.

As we concluded our interview with our usual question, "Can you imagine life without each other?" we got the answer we expected, but not a word was spoken. Their eyes welted up with tears, they gazed lovingly at each other for an extended period of time, and then they looked at us and smiled. No words were necessary. We knew their answer as well as we knew our own – lasting love 'til death do us part.

We know you will agree – Sandy and Pris are an inspiration to everyone. Their wonderful 61 years of marriage attest to the power of their relationship and the depth of their love. There is much to learn from these two lovebirds who have found "Lasting Love."

CHAPTER 38

The Look of Love in Brazil

One of the endearing characteristics of life in Brazil is the focus on the family.

IN RIO DE JANEIRO WE SAW the look of love from two lovebirds who have been in love since they were eight years old.

We had the great pleasure of interviewing Attilio Borriello and his bride of 51 years, Arlette. And trust us when we say this – they look like love! They are the look of love.

Attilio and Arlette are from San Lorenzo, Minas Gerais, Brazil, the third largest metropolitan area of the country and about a four-hour drive from Rio. They were in Rio visiting family, and we were introduced to them by their 23-year-old granddaughter, Cristiana.

We were blessed by the opportunity to interview them today over lunch at A Garota de Ipanema (*The Girl from Ipanema*) restaurant. Let us say up front, Attilio and Arlette are a near perfect match for the profile of successful marriage we have found in our travels around the world. In fact, their marital relationship of nearly 52 years is a mirror image of the long-time, successfully married couples we have interviewed over the years. They are what love is!

Over their 51 years of marriage they have birthed three children and are the proud grandparents of six grandchildren. They speak often and adoringly of their extended family.

In fact, one of the endearing characteristics of life in Brazil is the focus on the family. Many have told us that the principle reason the divorce rate in Brazil is only 20% is because of the strength of the family. Divorce is certainly allowable in Brazil, but with the loving support of the extended family, it is not the choice of first resort for most Brazilians, as it often is for many who live in the USA.

But as in all marriages, the most important determiner of success and longevity is the relationship between husband and wife. That relationship, in the end, trumps everything else. In the case of Attilio and Arlette, their relationship is amongst the most loving and supportive relationships we have ever witnessed. Our interview with them reinforced everything we have learned about successful marriage over the years.

In a nutshell, here is what makes their marriage work so well:

First and foremost they love each other deeply. You can see it in their eyes. You can see it in the way they lovingly and adoringly gazed at each other during the course of our interview with them. And you could see it in the way their eyes teared up when we asked what we have come to believe is the most important and telling question about the best marriages – "Can you imagine life without each other?" Their answer to this question was an emphatic "No!" Attilio went on to report that he "Doesn't ever want to think about it!" To these two lovebirds "death to us part" is the only way their marriage on Earth will ever end. They have committed their lives, their love, and their sacred honor until the end of time.

Secondly, Attilio and Arlette, learned early on in their relationship that to disagree from time to time is natural, even in the best marriages, but to escalate the disagreements into heated arguments is to be avoided at all costs. They have mastered the art of compromise. They have learned that a raised voice only exacerbates their occasional disagreement over an issue. Arlette reported that they both have learned to back away when they disagree over something and come back to the discussion later when the emotion of the moment has dissipated. Wonderful advice, don't you think?

And there is no question about it – Attilio and Arlette are best friends! They were friends long before they got married and have sustained that friendship throughout their marriage.

When asked to describe his friend, Arlette, Attilio used words like, "wonder woman," "my wonderful friend," "the best woman in the world," and "a strong person." Arlette described Attilio as her "best friend," "her hero," "her lover," "her everything!" The endearing terms about their friendship flowed from their lips. Their friendship is truly, "A Beautiful Love Story," the name they reported to us they would give to a book written about their enduring marriage.

Truth is, there is so much we could write about our new friends. There is so much we could say about them and their love for each other. But for now, we will summarize what they believe to be the most important reasons for the amazing success of their marriage over the years beyond the previously stated reasons.

Share and do many things together; always try to look your best for each other; be respectful of each other unfailingly; endeavor to interject variety and spice into your relationship; help each other to stay healthy (the right foods, annual physical exams, properly taking medications, etc.); share life's burdens; remember the special moments together; talk about anything and everything with your spouse; and above all else, touch each other often during each and every day. We would call this advice, advice to live by!

One final note to share – when Attilio and Arlette celebrated their 50th Wedding Anniversary (their Golden Anniversary) their family gave them a big celebration party at the JW Marriott Hotel on Copacabana Beach in Rio de Janeiro. Their room number was 714. Our room for our stay in Rio was 714! In addition, their granddaughter, Cristiana, works at the Marriott and checked us in and arranged for our interview with her grandparents. And the parallels continue – our daughter's name is Kristina. We think there is a good omen in there somewhere!

CHAPTER 39

Marriage Caribbean Style

These two lovebirds broke the trend many years ago and are a living portrait of love and marriage, Caribbean style.

HERE WE SIT GAZING AT the beautiful turquoise blue ocean from our perch on the balcony of our room at the Marriott Casa Magna in Cancun, Quintana Roo, Mexico. We are conducting interviews with successfully married couples in Mexico as we continue our travels around the world searching for the best marriages.

Today we had the pleasure of interviewing Isabel and Luis, two lovebirds who have been married for 33 years. They come from very different backgrounds but are very much in love with each other.

Luis grew up terribly poor in a small town in Mexico just to the west Leona Vicario. While his beginnings were humble, he has done well for himself and his family over the years. He has recently become the general manager for a resort hotel in the Caribbean, no small accomplishments for a boy who grew up with 10 siblings in a wooden pole hut with a dirt floor and a palm leaf thatched roof.

Most of us can only imagine what it was like to grow up that poor in a community where there is very little opportunity. Luis cut wood stakes at an early age and sold them to other families to burn for cooking and for keeping their homes warm at night. We were so curious about the little town he grew up in that we rented a car and drove to it earlier this week. It doesn't look like much has changed over the years. And those thatched palm leave roofs still adorn the modest huts with the dirt floors for many of the village residents. Luis has, indeed, come a long way.

Isabel had a different upbringing. Her father would be considered rich by most any standard. The view from her bedroom growing up was the beautiful turquoise colored ocean of the Caribbean Sea near Playa del Carmen, Quintana Roo, Mexico. Her father was a land developer along the Mexican Riviera by the Caribbean Ocean. He got in on the ground floor of a series of resorts that now dot the white sands of the Caribbean Ocean from Cancun to Tulum. Tourism is now the number one industry in this part of Mexico and Isabel's father got very rich developing those luxury resorts.

As you can imagine, the first time Luis and Isabel met they paid little attention to each other beyond a nod of the head when a friend of one of her brothers, Artemio, introduced them at a local Mercado one Saturday afternoon in Playa del Carmen, where Isabel shopped and Luis worked at a local hotel washing dishes.

Over time, this daughter of a wealthy land developer and this son of a pauper began to cross paths more frequently at various locations around town. And as curious as it might sound, they began, as Luis says, "making eyes at each other!" One warm Caribbean afternoon Luis asked this beautiful rich girl if she would go out with him and for some unexplainable reason according to Luis, she said yes!

Given the traditions of the time, Isabel's father would certainly object strenuously if he found out his daughter was dating a dishwasher. In her father's day, the families of the bride and groom arranged the marriage. The thought of a rich girl marrying a poor man was simply out of the question! Luis and Isabel knew that, but their love for each other grew every time they were together and grew even stronger when they were apart.

So you are asking yourself, "What is the rest of this story?" Did love triumph over family traditions? Did Luis marry Isabel over the objections of her father? Well, the truth is, Isabel's father loved her deeply and while he had great apprehension about her daughter's choice of a poor dishwasher for a husband, he did see great promise in Luis. In fact, he was quite impressed with Luis' intelligence and industriousness.

More importantly, he trusted and respected his daughter's judgment and as he frequently said, his daughter "was just like his wife" – strong, independent, a mind of her own – and he admired his daughter for being the same! In a country where men often ruled the roost after marriage, Isabel's father was a non-traditionalist. He admired strong women and could not stand in the way of his daughter's desires when it came to the man in her life. Luis was a good, decent, and honorable young man and if his daughter wanted to marry him, that was good enough for her father.

The wedding was lovely and for a marriage between rich and poor, it was a marriage to remember. The guest list was long and represented all the social classes of Mexico. The rich and famous met the poor and the underprivileged. And in the end, they all danced the night away to the sounds of the best mariachi band in Playa del Carmen! It seems that in the end, people are just people, irrespective of their socio-economic class. The marriage of Luis and Isabel is a testament to that.

Now, 33 years later, Luis and Isabel are still madly in love. They have succeeded where most similar cross-social class marriages in Mexico have failed. Their marriage has taught them much about the power of love, the importance of family, and the lessons of strength and conviction. These two lovebirds broke the trend many years ago and are a living portrait of love and marriage, Caribbean style.

Simple things matter in love and marriage. Choosing the one you love for love tops the list.

CHAPTER 40

A Golden Anniversary with a Dancing Twist

Your new dancing partner can be just around the next twirl at the local dance club!

TODAY WE WERE TOLD delightful story about life and love, and dancing. The story was apparently reported on the CBS Evening News and shared with us by a colleague. We heard a similar story a few months ago during a conversation with a couple we were interviewing. We will change the names in our story to protect the innocent. And you'll see why.

It seems that Mary was married to Ned for 50 years. They celebrated their Golden Anniversary together. Mary loved Ned and Ned loved Mary. It was a marriage success story. And while their marriage was a happy one, it had a tragic ending – Ned died.

Ned's death for a couple married for 50 years is probably not all that unusual or unexpected. At his death, Ned was 88 and Mary was

85. The sad truth is, people die. And often times the one you love deeply, dies. It is part of the cycle of life. Sad, but true.

But this story has a twist to it. You see, as committed as Mary was to Ned and as much as she loved him, her life with Ned for all those many years left her with an unaddressed beef about him. He didn't fulfill all her needs.

You see, Mary loves to dance. It was and has been her passion for most of her life. She reports that she dreamed about her "Knight in dancing armor" for most of her life. She would find her dancing man and they would dance the night away. You have heard about the "golden slipper" at the ball (a dance), well, this was a story about the dancing shoes.

When she married Ned, she soon discovered that he was not a dancer at all. In fact, he didn't dance with her during their 50 years of marriage! Not once. She never went dancing. Again, a sad story, but true.

But this story has a dancing twist. When Ned died, Mary met a new man. We shall call him George. George had a passion for dancing. And when they met at a dance hall in Oklahoma, it was love at *first dance.*

Mary had found her dancing man after all these years. And dance they did. They danced and danced and danced and danced!

There is something magical about dancing. As our Texas friend says, "You can learn a lot about love by dancing." The case of Mary and Ned, and now the dancing man, George, illustrates his point very well we think.

Now the story gets really interesting. According to Mary, her new man is a dancing king. George loves Mary and Mary loves George. Through their dancing, Mary at 88 and George at 83, are considering getting married. Dancing has done it again! George and Mary are getting ready to Tango again!

Here's the "dancing" twist to this story – Mary and George have been living together for nearly a year now – and they are ***not*** married. George says they were taught better, but at their age, "What's the rush? We will get married soon enough!" When you are in your late 80's, we call that great optimism! Life and love – saved by dancing!

The next time you are feeling down and blue, and out of love, just remember the story of Mary and George. Life and love can begin again when you are in your 80's. Love can begin again after you have enjoyed your Golden Anniversary with someone you loved for so many years who leaves you through death.

Sometimes those we love die. Sometimes a marriage ends for no reason other than death. But always remember this – true love can be found again. Your new dancing partner can be just around the next twirl at the local dance club!

Go dancing tonight. You never know.

CHAPTER 41

We'd Do It All Over Again!

And when all is said and done, you will say,
"I would do it all over again."

IN PROVIDENCE, RHODE ISLAND, 300 married couples said, "I do," all over again. Isn't that wonderful! The participating couples were married from 25 to 70 years and loved each other so much that they chose to reaffirm their commitment to each other by renewing their marriage vows, and in a very public way. They promised once more, "To have and to hold, from this day forward, for better, for worse, for richer, for poorer, in sickness or in health, to love and to cherish 'till death do us part."

This "good news" story caught our attention when we saw a video clip on one of the nightly news shows about it. It struck a chord with us because for nearly three decades we have interviewed successfully married couples that were married between 30 and 77 years.

One of the questions in our interview protocol asks the couple we are interviewing if they would marry each other all over again. The answer tells you a lot about the quality of their relationship and the success of their marriage, and it provides a true testament to their love for each other.

With the happily married couples, the answer is nearly always a resounding, "yes!" On the other hand, for those that equivocate, you get a sense that all is not well with their relationship. The successfully married couples we have interviewed over the years gave their lives, their love, and their sacred honor to each other and would not hesitate to make that same commitment again.

You see, true love ***is*** forever. We know that skeptics abound when it comes to this notion, but many of them miss the most important point of its meaning. Let us explain.

When people fall in love do they say, "I will fall in love with you until somebody else comes along I love more." Do they say, "You are the love of my life today, but I will look for a new one tomorrow." Worse yet, just imagine someone setting a time limit on their love – "I will love you for ten years and then will move on to another lover." Sounds silly when you think about it, huh?

Why commit your love to someone if you don't think it will last forever? True love, it seems to us, is all about commitment. You can't truly love someone if you do not believe your relationship to be permanent. If you feel that it is not, what you are feeling is probably not real love but infatuation or some other emotion that disguises itself as love.

Take a look at the chapter *How Will I Know I Am In Love?* to see the indicators of real love. In that chapter we outline Seven Categories of answers to this most important of all questions about love and relationships – how do you know you are in love. When you truly know you are in love, you are ready to make the commitment to another person. But that is only half the story – the other person has to feel that way as well. It does, as we often say, take two to Tango!

We have learned many lessons over the years about lasting love. Long-lasting and successful relationships begin and end with unqualified and undying love and commitment. To think otherwise is to set yourself up for failure in love, and life.

May the love of your life share their life with you until the end. And when all is said and done, you will say, "I would do it all over again."

Here's to lasting love.

Love Well Forever!

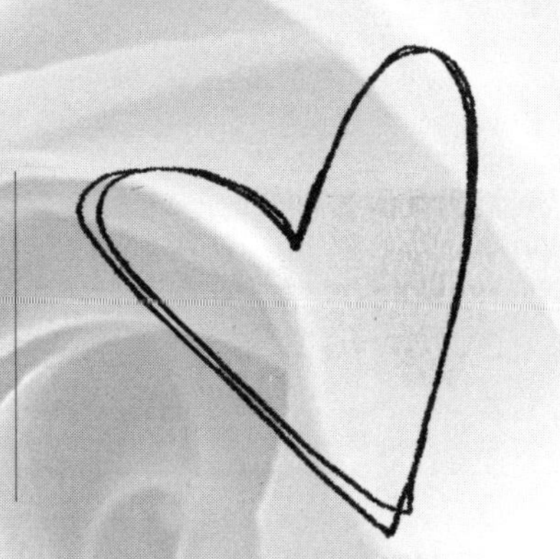

HOW CAN MARRIAGE SURVIVE CHALLENGES?

SIMPLE THINGS MATTER

CHAPTER 42

Debunking the Divorce Rate Myth

But the truth is, the suggestion that there is a 50% divorce rate in American is simply wrong, wrong, wrong!

LET'S FACE IT, A LOT OF couples contemplating marriage get discouraged by the oft-quoted statistic that 50% of marriages in America end in divorce. Who could blame them? Who wants to get into relationships where there is the expectation of failure half the time! But the truth is, the suggestion that there is a 50% divorce rate in American is simply wrong, wrong, wrong! We would like to de-bunk that myth, that fiction, that urban legend!

Where did such a notion come from? What could be the motivation of groups and individuals that promulgate such a falsehood? Do they want to discourage traditional marriage? Do they have a political agenda? Have they simply offered a conclusion based on their faulty analysis of the available data? Or worse yet, have they intentionally misrepresented what we know about marriage and divorce in America in order to undermine this great social institution?

The answer we guess is probably all of the above to some extent. Clearly, it is hard to get into the hearts and minds of human beings. Without a doubt, it is difficult to determine the motivations of others. So, we will resist talking about the motives of folks and simply deal with the facts about divorce in America. And here are the facts.

First of all, the divorce rate is not nearly as high as it is often reported in the popular media. We need to change that perception because it can be a discouraging message to those contemplating marriage.

The divorce rate in America is not 50% for first-time marriages, period! For example, most experts we have talked to believe the rate is closer to 40%. We ourselves have estimated the rate in previous writings at somewhere between 35% and 40%. A 2001 survey by researcher George Barna estimated that 34% of American's who have ever been married have ever been divorced. Several studies we have reviewed actually estimated the divorce rate to be less than 20%. It is our considered opinion that the 20% and less figures are too low, but one thing is clear – more than 60% of marriages are successful!

Pinning down the exact divorce rate in America is certainly complicated. Many studies have been done, many numbers crunched, and many conclusions drawn. But the truth of the matters is, the national per capita divorce rate has declined steadily since its peak in 1981 and is now ***at its lowest level since 1970.*** The fact that the per capita divorce has declined should be cause for celebration.

Secondly, there are a number of factors that can reduce the divorce rate and rather than dwelling on the perceived chances of failure of a marriage we should be looking for reasons why most marriages do not fail – do not end in divorce.

Over the years we have seen a positive trend developing and it is highly encouraging to us. It is clear to us that more and more couples are working harder and harder to make their marriage work. They are investing solid efforts at strengthening their marriage. They read books like ours on the subject (*Golden Anniversaries: The Seven Secrets of Successful Marriage*), they participate in marriage enrichment programs, they seek counseling from a qualified professional counselor or psychologist, and they learn to do the ***simple things*** that make marriage work each and every day of their lives together.

The good news – more and more couples are committed to making their marriage work! In a society that is often characterized as "a disposable society," marriage should not be one of those things we routinely dispose of! As we have said many times before, not all marriages are worth saving, but ***most are and can be saved!***

And thirdly, we need to debunk the many myths about how to ensure a successful relationship. And here's one to begin with. Despite the belief of many, living together while not married does not necessarily promote a happy and successful relationship. For example, the Centers for Disease Control reported that there is only a 20% chance that first marriages will end in divorce in the first five years. On the other hand, the separation rate in the first five years for those cohabiting is a ***whopping 49%!*** These data seem to fly in the face of those who suggest that giving marriage a trial run or just cohabiting instead of marrying at all, is the way to go. It seems these advice givers need to check their facts about what works.

There is a corollary to the aforementioned notion about living together. Some researchers have reported that the highest risk factor for divorce is moving in together prior to marriage! Couples who do this have a ***far greater risk of divorce.*** In fact, couples who cohabitat before marriage – who give their "marriage" a trial run – have a divorce rate reported as high as 85%. Talk about the destruction of a myth!

We know that second and third marriages have high failure rates. Most studies report that second marriages have about a two out of three chance of failure – third marriages about a 75% chance. These second and third marriages (as well as those married four or more times) get lumped into divorce equations that are often reported. The simple truth is, the "impact rate" of divorce – those individuals that divorce ***actually impacts*** – is clearly much lower than the oft-reported rate of 50%. Those married for the first time just need to learn to get it right the first time!

So what are the factors that have major implications for the risk of divorce? Barbara Whitehead and David Popenoe in their book entitled *The State of Our Unions* (2004) reported the following:

1. ***Couples with annual incomes over $50,000 (vs. under $25,000) have a reduced risk of divorce of 30%.*** The message here is that couples contemplating marriage would be well advised to have income-producing jobs with stability before they get married.

2. ***Couples who have a baby seven months or more after marriage (vs. before marriage) have a reduced risk of divorce of 24%.*** The message here should be clear – bring children into the world when your marriage is ready.

*3. **Couples who are 25 years of age (vs. under 18) have a 24% less risk of divorce.*** The American divorce rate has been going down since 1981 because people in love are waiting longer to get married. Gaining education, experience, and the wisdom that comes with age will certainly contribute to the success of a marriage.

*4. **Couples that consider themselves religious or spiritual (vs. not) are 14% less likely to get divorced.*** Faith and spirituality contribute to the sense of ***oneness*** felt by successfully married couples.

*5. **Couples who have some college (vs. high-school dropout) have a 13% less chance of divorce.*** Education almost always leads to enlightenment and understanding, and more tolerance for the views of others. All are so critically important in successful marriages.

In summary, reasonably well-educated couples with a decent income, who are religious or spiritual, who wait awhile to have children, who come from intact families, and who marry later in life (25 and beyond), have a greatly reduced chance of divorce.

The American divorce rate is much lower than often reported. And considering that the average American has a 90% chance of being married at least once in their lifetime, it is nice to know that there is much we can do as individuals and as couples in love to make marriage work – to make marriage successful.

CHAPTER 43

Seven Secrets to Avoiding the Seven-Year Itch

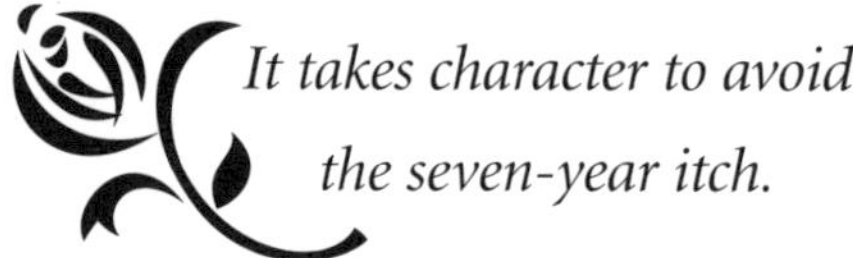
It takes character to avoid the seven-year itch.

THE U.S. CENSUS BUREAU issued a press release entitled "Most People Make Only One Trip Down the Aisle, But First Marriages Shorter." Needless to say, the article grabbed our attention immediately since we write about this stuff all the time.

There were a number of interesting highlights reported in the press release but the one that piqued our interest the most was the following: "On average, first marriages that end in divorce last about eight years." This phenomenon has often been referred to as the "*Seven-Year Itch.*"

First, a little background. Most aficionados of the *Seven-Year Itch* trace it back to a play by the same name written by one George

Axelrod. His three-act play was first performed on Broadway in New York City in 1952. Three years later, a movie by the same title starring the late, great Marylyn Monroe was released by 20th Century Fox.

Before we get to the "plot" of this article, we also wanted to remind you that the *Seven-Year Itch* has also been associated with an itchy and irritating skin rash that has been reported to last for up to seven years. Frankly, this notion is very closely related to what happens in a number of marriages as we explain in the paragraphs to follow.

In the most basic sense, the *Seven-Year Itch* is the inclination of some to become unfaithful to their spouse after seven years of marriage. Most of these marriages end in the 8th year (see above).

In the play and the movie of the same title, a married man by the name of Richard is currently reading a book about to be published by his company entitled "*7-Year Itch.*" The book offers the notion that a large percentage of men have extra-marital affairs after seven years of marriage; hence, the *Seven-Year Itch.* At the same time he is reading the book, he meets a young blond television model. As you might imagine, the plot thickens!

As the just released Census data suggest, there just might be something to the *Seven-Year Itch* when it comes to marriage. The more basic question is, how do you stay faithful to the one you love and keep your loving relationship healthy and strong so it survives the ups, the downs, and the temptations present in all relationships at one time or another.

We have written about the importance of honesty, trust, and faithfulness in love and marriage in the chapter entitled *Character in Love and Marriage.* It takes character to avoid the seven-year itch.

We believe we have learned much from our research on successful marriage and loving relationships and would like to share some of our findings with you within the context of this conversation about the *Seven-Year Itch.* Here they are in a nutshell.

The first of the seven rules for avoiding the *Seven-Year Itch* is this – understand that infatuation with another person and the temptation to betray the trust of the one you love is a perfectly normal feeling when it comes to love and marriage. Getting hitched to another person doesn't make you less human. It does, in many ways, make you more human – more in touch with your feelings and emotions. Accept the feelings.

Rule number two is – do not under any circumstances act on those infatuation and temptation impulses until you have taken the time to fully think through the consequences if you make that choice. Cheating on your spouse or loved one can be and often is deadly to your relationship. Rebuilding trust is nearly impossible after committing such an indiscretion.

The third rule to avoid the *Seven-Year Itch* is to recognize that continuing and recurring fantasies and infatuations about another person is a strong indicator of something amiss in your relationship with your spouse or lover. These feelings are often associated with a deep-seated problem in your relationship that must be addressed before it is too late.

The fourth rule – the "turn the corner rule" as we like to refer to it – is to address the issue head-on with your loving partner. Failure to do so will doom your relationship to the ash-heap of lost love. There is pain to be sure when you address the issues that are destroying your loving relationship, but to not do so will be even more painful, we guarantee it!

Rule five is a tough one. You and your lover may discover in rule four that love is tough. It is sometimes unforgiving. Frankly, sometimes you determine that your loving relationship is lost. But more likely you discover that you truly love your spouse and that you cannot imagine life without them. You find out what so many before have discovered – you love your mate so much you cannot under any circumstances let them go. You must save this relationship by committing to the hard work it will take to rebuild the love.

Which is why rule six is so critically important. Rule six says, seek help! Find some neutral party to talk to. Sometimes couples turn to a marriage counselor. Others turn to "self-help" websites like www.SelfGrowth.com. Truth is, much of what you need to learn can be self-taught. You can learn to do what you have to do to make your relationship work by reading what others, including us, have discovered. Being educators at heart, we especially like the latter. More often than not, you can learn so much about yourself and your loving relationship by "discovering" what others have already learned!

All of this leads to rule seven. Rule seven is a simple rule, really. At it's essence, it says to us that sometimes we have to "fish or cut bait." The reality is that some marriages and loving relationships cannot be saved. They are doomed. They must end to the mutual benefit of both and to the many that are affected by the relationship. It is time to move on. But in the end, an examination of your relationship will hopefully reveal that your relationship is worth saving. More often than not, it can be saved. You should always work towards that end if you are to avoid the *Seven-Year Itch.*

We offer these seven rules to help you avoid the *Seven-Year Itch* so you can be one of those happy and successfully married couples who celebrate their golden anniversaries together.

CHAPTER 44

Love In Tough Economic Times

There is a natural tendency in tough times to blame the one you love for your collective misfortune.

FOR THE PAST SEVERAL MONTHS the Stock Market has been in decline, the unemployment rate has gone up, and home ownership has taken a dip. Sometimes, watching the evening news causes one to wonder if the good old USA is in decline, if the financial state of America has caused marriages to crumble, love to decline, and people to forget the greatness of the nation we live in.

We would offer that while times are tougher than normal, the best marriages and love affairs will sustain the test of time for all the right reasons – during good or bad times the best loving relationships almost always survive. And we know why!

The truth is, the economy of the USA is on a roller coaster ride, but in an historical sense, there is nothing particularly unusual about the current economic turmoil. We have been here before. There have been worse times

The more important question through all this is, "How do we as a married couple, or lovers engaged in a loving relationship, make sure we sustain our love affair through all this turmoil, through all this uncertainty?"

As we stated so clearly in our writing and interviews, people in love must talk sense when dealing with their dollars. Here's what we mean.

Balancing the family budget requires teamwork. It requires common goals. It most certainly requires family support. People in love support each other through thick and thin – through tough times and uncertainty.

People in love don't blame, castigate, or chastise each other in tough economic times. They work together to make ends meet and to prepare for tomorrow.

There is a natural tendency in tough times to blame the one you love for your collective misfortune. There is, sadly, the desire to find a scapegoat when times get tough. There is, unfortunately, the need to find someone to blame when your economic fortunes go south. But it doesn't have to be that way because the truth is, there usually is no one to blame for your misfortune.

People in love don't wallow in self-pity. They grab "the bull by the horns" and work for solutions – recognizing that running a household is not easy. Making a family work is, clearly, difficult even in the best of times. But the unequivocal truth is this – if you don't view your relationship as one requiring teamwork, all is lost. If you don't work together to address head-on the economic challenges of your relationship with each other, there is little hope of success.

Whether you lost your job due to downsizing or whether you had to take a pay cut to keep the job you have, always remember this, what sustains your relationship is being in love with someone you trust – someone you would trust with you love, your sacred honor, and with your life.

In summary, here are the seven most important actions you can take to protect your love during tough economic times:

1. Approach all financial problems with teamwork. These are after all ***our*** problems not my problems and ***your*** problems.

2. Communicate openly about all financial issues facing your relationship. You are in this together.

3. Set common goals for resolving your financial setbacks. Agreeing on a course of action provides the clarity of purpose necessary for finding a solution.

4. Don't blame each other if things go south. The blame game doesn't work in love and marriage.

5. Don't wallow in self-pity; it is a wasted emotion. No problem has ever been solved by feeling sorry for yourself or your situation.

6. Take action today to begin addressing your financial issues together. When you are in love being the Lone Ranger doesn't earn you bonus points.

7. Celebrate each time you have a financial success such as paying off a credit card or finding a way to cut expenses. Fiscal responsibility is a virtue.

Times do occasionally get tough, but here's the bottom line – if you have a loving and trusting relationship with someone, believe in that. If you love someone completely, then understand that your true love will sustain you through the best of times, and the worst of times.

The sour economic conditions of the country will pass. But always remember this – your love for each other will sustain you. Having someone to love and someone who loves you, is the greatest gift. True love is always sustained through the good times and the bad.

These times of uncertainty shall pass.

C H A P T E R 2

Character in Love and Marriage

Character in a successful marriage
or relationship does matter,
and character is about trust.

In case you didn't know it, there is a character element in love and loving relationships. People who say they love each other and then cheat on their spouse or lover, or lie to them on a regular basis, aren't really in love. Oh, many think they are, but they really are not. People who love each other have character when it comes to their marriage or relationship.

In our interviews with couples that had a successful marriage we are always struck by their undying trust in each other. They literally trust each other with their lives, their fortune, and their sacred honor. The words they use to describe the one they love more often than not include words and expressions like trust, honesty, loyalty, respects me, admires me, always there for me, never lets me down, truthful, and never lies to me. Their trust for each other is about as complete as you can get. And when we ask couples in love during our interviews to place, in an overall sense, where their relationship is on a 10-point scale with 10 being "Absolute Trust," without exception, they say "10!" Isn't that wonderful? Remarkable? These are the couples that will celebrate their golden anniversaries together!

Trust is not something all loving relationships start with. For some couples the trust becomes complete in a few years. For others, it takes awhile. But one thing is for sure; happy and successful marriages and relationships survive and thrive on the basis of this trust. Trust is so pervasive in their relationship that they never give it a second thought. They expect it. It's always there. It is part of the fabric of their marriage.

There is one thing you can take to the bank – all people in love have faced temptations in their relationship. The pretty girl in the restaurant captures your fancy. The handsome man walking down the street draws your attention. The flirt at work is tempting at times. And, we will dare say, sometimes in every relationship you think about slipping in the sack with some of the beautiful people you meet. But here's where it stops – these are only fleeting moments of passing fancy. These are the moments of momentary lust for another human being that are not acted on. Why? People in love who are happy in their relationships control their urges because they know that while a moment of sexual fantasy is healthy and normal, following through and enjoying sexual satisfaction with someone other than their mate – cheating on their mate – is destructive to the loving and trusting relationship between them. It's okay to have sexual urges and fantasies regarding another person, but to act on them ruins all that trust. It destroys the ties that bind.

Couples who are truly in love in their relationship know that a few moments of sexual satisfaction can NEVER replace the loving, trusting, and caring relationship they have developed with their mate. As someone once said to us, "I have a marriage license but I didn't give up my looking license!" Admiring others in intimate ways is normal and healthy. But acting on those urges has ruined many a marriage and many a loving relationship.

Those wonderful couples we have interviewed resist these normal urges and temptations of life because they know their relationship is so much more important to them. Destroying the trust between them causes the foundation of their marriage to crumble.

Character in a successful marriage or relationship does matter, and character is about trust. Being honest and trustworthy is at the heart of all the best loving relationships we have studied. It really is a 10 on a 10-point scale. In our estimation, character is the foundation of true love! This is one of the most important lessons we have learned.

CHAPTER 46

Nurturing Your Children And Your Marriage

You thought your marriage
was nearly perfect –
And Then…Along Came Kids.

KIDS! WE LOVE THEM. We cherish them. They bring joy to our lives. When we have children in a marriage, we understand finally, and once and for all, what eternity means. While we are not immortal, we learn the meaning of everlasting life when we are blessed with children. They make us feel like we will live through time. We carry on through them. We know that through them our lives will have meaning beyond our time on this earth.

But our children are also a pain in the butt! They challenge us. They taunt us. They demand much from us. They argue with us.

They divide us. They unite us. They run up one heck of a child-care bill!

On the other hand, most successful marriages with children wouldn't want it any other way. They know that without a doubt, their children enrich their lives in innumerable ways. They value their children immensely. But be clear regarding this – successfully married couples with children understand the challenges they pose to a blissful and romantic marital relationship.

You thought your marriage was nearly perfect – ***And Then…Along Came Kids.*** To quote Nora Ephron in *Heartburn:* "Having a first child is like throwing a hand grenade into a marriage." When you are responsible for the care of your children, you will, without a doubt, take on some enormous stresses.

After more than 26 years of research around the world interviewing successfully married couples, one of our principal conclusions is – ***the quality of the relationship between husband and wife trumps everything else in a marriage!*** Get it right and good things follow. Get it wrong and lots of bad things often happen!

And you know why? Without a positive, loving, and thriving relationship between mom and dad, children often don't prosper, they are not well-adjusted, they don't do well in school, and they are not as healthy, both physically and mentally.

Our research over the years suggests that there are a number of useful tips that you can use to not only deal with the enormous stress of caregiving, but also strengthen your marriage at the same time. These tips appear on the surface to be simple, but in love, marriage and raising children the "Simple Things Matter".

Tips for Moms to Strengthen Your Marriage:

1. ***Share openly with each other about feelings, emotions and stresses as they relate to caring for your children.*** In times of

stress the tendency is to keep everything bottled up inside or explode at the slightest disagreement. However, this approach will not work if you want your marriage to survive and thrive. In successful marriages there are No Sacred Cows. Simply speaking, happily married couples talk about everything. All subjects are fair game. They trust each other. They rely on each other's good judgment. They depend upon each other for truth and straight talk. They share insights about everything – the good, the bad and the ugly. They are each other's best friends.

2. ***Make a conscious effort to keep the flame of your love affair alive with each other everyday.*** Can you rattle off a list of activities, topics and places you and your spouse include in your personal book of fun and romance? Have you found what clears your mind and gives you an unobstructed view of your world together? What type of priority do you place on making time for fun and romance with each other in your hectic lives? If you cannot answer these questions easily, you need to start today by carving out time to have a romantic date with each other, bring home flowers, get a hotel room, go for a long walk together, drink a bottle of wine watching the sunset, write a love note, and snuggle in bed a little longer in the morning.

3. ***Don't blame each other when things get tough, as casting blame never solved a problem.*** The blame game doesn't work in love and marriage. It is destructive. There is a natural tendency in tough times to blame the one you love for your collective misfortune, but people in love don't blame, castigate, or chastise each other in challenging times. The truth is, there usually is no one to blame for the situation. Someone has to take care of the children and the job just fell to you.

4. ***Don't wallow in self-pity; it is a wasted emotion.*** No problem has ever been solved by feeling sorry for yourself or your situation. Trying to pretend you are the perfect super mom while you are totally overwhelmed, can only result in the wasted emotion of self-pity and even more stress. Successful couples grab "the bull by the horns" and work for solutions – recognizing that running a household is not easy. Making a family work is, clearly, difficult even in the best of times and even more challenging when you are the caring for your children.

5. ***Enhance your love relationship by providing each other occasional time for privacy and aloneness.*** The recognition of the absolute need for privacy and aloneness is, in our judgment after analyzing thousands of interviews, critical to successful marriages. The amount of time available to satisfy these two needs varies from one marriage to another and from one marriage partner to another, and can increase during times of stress. We live such hectic lives at work, at home and when raising children that the time to be alone with our own thoughts is paramount to our ability to engage in meaningful communication with each other. The quality of communication can only be enhanced between the two of you after refreshing your mind and spirit with alone time. You have to belong to yourself before you can belong to others. Unfortunately, moms spend so much time caring for others that they don't take care their own needs. You can't take good care of others if you don't take good care of yourself.

You brought your children into this world with the greatest of love and now you have to balance all of the stresses they bring to your marriage. Your children won't be with your forever, so enjoy them while you can. Believe it or not they grow up oh so quickly. Cherish those precious moments but remember – ***the quality of the relationship between mom and dad trumps everything else.***

CHAPTER 47

Love By Bullying Never Works

Letting a bully win is a bad idea.

DON'T YOU JUST HATE bullies! They try to get what they want by bullying you, by intimidating you, and by making you feel inferior to them. If you are like us, this NEVER works! Yet, so many good folks succumb to the bully. And we wonder why?

So what is a bully? In the simplest terms, a bully is someone who can't get what he/she wants through normal means. What they want is power. When you deny them that power they resort to forceful means to get what they want.

Here is how it works in love and marriage. One of the folks in the relationship wants something – be it a new car, a new apartment, a new dishwasher, or a new toy of some variety. The other person involved in the relationship does not. As you might guess, all heck breaks loose!

The "bully" in the relationship must get what he/she wants. So instead of acting rationally (i.e., Do we have enough money to pay for this?), the bully resorts to name-calling (i.e., You are always keeping me from buying things!"), intimidation ("If you don't let me buy this I am walking out the door."), or they resort to making you feel inferior (i.e., How could someone like you be so stupid?").

If you are like most people, you would rather "have peace." So in the interest of maintaining harmony in your relationship, you fall prey to the bullying – you give them what they want.

But here is the deal – this strategy never works! You give them what they want and they then do it to you again! You always succumb to their wishes. You always lose. Letting a bully win is a bad idea. Finding the courage to stand up to a bully is perhaps the only way to effectively stop the bullying once and for all.

Truth is, real loving relationships are not about you and me, they are about US! They are about WE. As we are fond of saying, "It takes two to Tango." You cannot Tango by yourself. Until you learn this important lesson in your relationship, your relationship will be doomed to failure.

So, how do you handle the bully in your loving relationship?

CHAPTER 48

It is NOT Okay to Cheat on the One You Love

The truth is, if we all had our Summer of Love there would be no violence, no heartbreak, no disaffection, no scorn or hate—there would be only love and peace.

IT IS NOT OKAY TO CHEAT on the one you love and let's quit pretending that it is. Enough is enough! Character in love and marriage matters.

While we were driving to a television interview this morning we were listening to a local radio station. They had on an "expert" (and we use that term very lightly) who said, and we quote, "The only real loser in all of this is Eliot Spitzer, the Governor of New York." Imagine, a man cheats on his wife repeatedly and HE is the victim – he is the only loser? Please, give us a break! The victim in this whole sordid affair is his wife, Silda, and her three daughters. Let's make no mistake about that.

There are many troubling aspects of this particular case of marital infidelity that bother us well beyond Mr. Spitzer's many encounters with a prostitute. Perhaps the most egregious of all is his having the audacity to have his wife by his side as he declares his public shame for what he did. Imagine, it was not enough that he brought shame on himself and his family, but he had to publicly humiliate his wife again by having her "stand by her man." How sick is that? How sick is it that in the name of politics he would subject his wife to this further humiliation?

Silda Spitzer was betrayed once by her husband's sordid affairs with prostitutes, again by the public humiliation of "standing by her man," and again by her having to look her daughters in their eyes to explain the shame and betrayal their father had brought upon the house of Spitzer.

We have been reminded again and again that trust is at the very heart of all successful and long-lasting relationships between people who love each other. In fact, we were genuinely inspired by the words of these lovebirds about the importance of trust in their marriage.

The essence of our message is this – trust undergirds everything in a successful marriage and the violation of that trust – the betrayal of that trust – will, in the end, ruin most marriages that experience it. Think about it, is there a worst sin that a spouse could commit than to betray the trust and the sacred honor of their marriage – of their relationship with the one they purport to love? And the plain and simple fact is this – most marriages NEVER recover from this level of trauma to the relationship.

Don't kid yourself, when you make the decision to cheat on your spouse, you have made a decision that will almost always cause irreparable harm to your loving relationship – one from which your marriage and your family will never recover.

Contrary to what our aforementioned "expert" said on the radio this morning, the ones who are truly hurt by the actions of Governor Spitzer are his wife and his daughters. They experienced the ultimate betrayal. They will probably never fully recover.

In life and love, the simple things matter, and the simple truth is, violating the most sacred of all trusts between two human beings who love each other is the ultimate betrayal. Think about this before you cheat on your spouse, before you commit your love to another human being, and before you say "I do."

Character in marriage matters!

CHAPTER 49

Love by Dancing

A great relationship can be improved by simple acts. Just go dancing!

A TEXAS FRIEND OF OURS swears that great love comes to those who dance. And guess what, he makes a very compelling case!

In a nutshell, we have concluded that one of the seven secrets of a successful loving relationship is touching. If you pass the one you love 100 times a day, touch them! Touching acknowledges the presence of the one you love and tells them, "I love you so much I simply must touch you."

We base this finding about "touching" on our study of 15,000 years of successful marriage – marriages we studied across cultures and continents, across ethnicities, and across the socio-economic spectrum. Touching is a very important part of love. All successful loving relationships thrive on the human touch by the one they love and the one who loves them.

Dancing is a great example of touching. We have written endlessly about the Tango, a dance we call the "dance of love." When we traveled to Buenos Aires, Argentina recently we were blown away by the exotic and loving nature of the Tango. They dance it on the street, in Tango clubs like *Senor Tango*, and at home! In fact, we were so enamored with the Tango, we wrote a chapter in our book about it entitled "It Takes Two To Tango."

Now, here is where this all comes together. The great marriages and loving relationships we have studied demonstrate the power of touch in the loving relationship. Relationships that touch the most, ***love the most.*** We are convinced of that!

And secondly, we are absolutely convinced of this important axiom – it takes two to Tango. You cannot Tango by yourself. In so many ways, the Tango is the essence of so many successful loving relationships. In the best marriages and loving relationships we have studied, "I" and "me" and "you" becomes "we" and "us" and "our."

So you now see why dancing is such a great way to find love, to be in love, and to enjoy love. Our Texas friend is a smart guy!

Every loving relationships hits bumps in the road. Sometimes those bumps turn into earthquakes! The point is, even the best relationships have moments when they hit a wall – when they are full of despair and angst. In our opinion, based on years of research and observation, these periods strengthen these relationships. Do not despair!

Here is what you do next time your relationship is down and when your relationship has lost some of its romance – go dancing! Whatever your favorite music venue is, find it and go dancing.

Whether it is Big Band, Tango, Country Dancing, Samba, the Cha Cha, Disco, Waltz, Swing, or the Salsa, ***just go dancing!*** You will spend the night touching the one you love, sharing wonderful and sensual moments together, and regaining once again the magic of why you are in love because it does take Two to Tango.

Ah, Love by Dancing – is there anything better? And as we always say, in love and marriage the simple things matter. A great relationship can be improved by simple acts. Just go dancing!

CHAPTER 50

Caring for Aging Parents and Your Marriage

Our research over the years suggests that there are a number of useful tips that you can use to not only deal with the stress of caregiving, but also strengthen your marriage at the same time.

WE ARE "BABY-BOOMERS." Like some 80 million Americans, we were born during the period 1946-1964. We are that generation of Americans born to what former NBC anchor Tom Brokaw called, "The Greatest Generation." Our parents survived the Great Depression, won the Second World War, and by most accounts, saved the world and preserved democracy in a post-war era.

There is no doubt; the free world owes a great debt of gratitude to the Greatest Generation. Frankly, it is hard to imagine where we would be without their sacrifices and their contributions to the creation of modern day America – to the creation of the world we live in today. We owe our parents a lot; there is no doubt about that.

Like some of you, our parents are gone. Losing our respective parents was among the most difficult things we have had to cope with in our lives. But the undeniable truth of life is this – you will not get out of this world alive!

As we write this for you today, we are fully cognizant that the parents of the baby-boomers are dying by the hundreds everyday. People get old and they die. There is nothing mysterious going on here. The realities of life tell us that the inevitable is lurking on the horizon. But the good news, our parents are living longer and longer. We get to have them around for a greater portion of our lives than our parents had of their parents.

Having aging parents who might live into their 80's and 90's (and beyond) can, however, bring a whole new set of challenges to your own marriage. You will recall the challenges associated with having children enter your own marriage. Nora Ephron once said that having children was "like throwing a hand grenade into a marriage!" Having your aging parents move back into your marriage, whether in your home or theirs, can have much the same effect.

When you take on the responsibility of caring for aging parents you will, without a doubt, take on some enormous stresses. The many challenges of caring for aging parents will at times put unbelievable strain on your marital relationship. Our research over the years suggests that there are a number of useful tips that you can use to not only deal with the stress of caregiving, but also strengthen your marriage at the same time.

Tips for Caregivers to Strengthen Your Marriage:

1. ***Talk openly with each other about feelings, emotions and stresses as they relate to your care of aging parents.*** In times of stress the tendency is to keep everything bottled up inside or explode with the slightest disagreement. However, this approach will not work if you want your marriage to survive and thrive. In successful marriages there are *No Sacred Cows.* Simply speaking, happily married couples talk about everything. All subjects are fair game. They trust each other. They rely on each other's good judgment. They depend upon each other for truth and straight talk. They share insights about everything – the good, the bad and the ugly. They are each other's best friends.

2. ***Approach all financial challenges with teamwork and open communication.*** Balancing the family budget requires teamwork, especially when the added burden of taking care of aging parents comes your way. It requires common goals. It most certainly requires family support. People in love support each other through thick and thin – through tough times and uncertainty. The unequivocal truth is this – if you don't view your relationship as one requiring teamwork, all is lost. If you don't work together to address head-on the economic challenges of your relationship with each other when caring for an aging parent, there is little hope of success.

3. ***Don't blame each other when things get tough, as casting blame never solved a problem.*** The blame game doesn't work in love and marriage and it is destructive. There is a natural tendency in tough times to blame the one you love for your collective misfortune, but people in love don't blame, castigate, or chastise each other in challenging times. The truth is, there usually is no one to blame for the situation. Someone

has to take care of aging parents and the job just fell to you.

4. ***Don't wallow in self-pity; it is a wasted emotion.*** No problem has ever been solved by feeling sorry for yourself or your situation. Successful couples grab "the bull by the horns" and work for solutions – recognizing that running a household is not easy. Making a family work is, clearly, difficult even in the best of times and even more challenging when you are the caregiver for an aging parent.

5. ***Make a concerted effort to keep the flame of your love affair alive with each other everyday.*** Can you rattle off a list of activities, topics and places that you and your spouse include in your personal book of fun and romance? Have you found what clears your mind and gives you an unobstructed view of your world together? What type of priority do you place on making time for fun and romance with each other in your hectic lives? If you cannot answer these questions easily, you need to start today with carving out time to have a romantic date with each other, bring home flowers, get a hotel room, go for a long walk together, drink a bottle of wine watching the sunset, write a love note, and snuggle in bed a little longer.

6. ***Enhance your love relationship by providing each other occasional time for privacy and aloneness.*** The recognition of the absolute need for privacy and aloneness is, in our judgment after analyzing thousands of interviews, critical to successful marriages. The amount of time available to satisfy these two needs varies from one marriage to another and from one marriage partner to another, and can increase during times of stress. We live such hectic lives at work, at home and when caring for aging parents that the time to be alone with our own thoughts is paramount to our ability to engage in any meaningful communication. The quality of communication

can only be enhanced between the two of you after refreshing your mind and spirit with alone time. You have to belong to yourself before you can belong to others.

7. ***Remember that the "Simple Things Matter" in marriage and they need to be practiced each day.*** Twenty-six years of research on successful love and marriage has taught us many things, but first and foremost – no love has blossomed or been sustained without doing the "simple things." Big things don't matter until your relationship has mastered the art of doing the simple things day in and day out in your relationship with another human being whom you purport to love. Too often when we are engaged in stressful life altering situations such as caring for aging parents we forget to just do the "simple things" for the one we love the most. Try engaging in simple acts of kindness, always treating each other with courtesy, sharing a shower together, and hugging often. Trust us on this – if your relationship with the one you love has mastered the art of doing the simple things day in and day out, the likelihood of your relationship making it through the tough times are multiplied many times over. The point is, "simple things matter" and when you practice doing them, they accumulate. Simple acts of kindness add up.

Your parents cared for you. They took you through your tough times growing up and, like most parents, probably continued to provide support for you long after you left their home. Like many children of aging parents, it is now your time to return the favor.

Your parents deserve your love, your understanding, and your support in their time of need. Rather than accept this responsibility as a challenge, take it on as an opportunity to get closer to your parents and deepen your love for them. They won't be around forever. Enjoy them while you can.

CHAPTER 51

Sex Will Not Save Your Marriage

To single out sex is to blow its importance entirely out of proportion to its relevance to a great marriage.

H MY GOODNESS, WHAT NEXT?

We heard today that a minister in Grapevine, Texas plans to tell his congregation in his sermon that he wants married couples to have sex all week long. He says that God may have rested on the seventh day, but he wants married couples to have sex every day for a week!

He goes on to say, "I won't be dressed in pajamas" while delivering his sermon while sitting on a bed. In these days of financial crisis, debates over same-sex marriage, and the like, it's time, he says, to turn the "whining" into "whoopee."

The question is, where do you start with debunking such a ridiculous notion. Let us count the ways!

For starters, we all know that good sex can be fun, romantic, exciting, and something that makes most consenting adults feel warm and fuzzy all over. Over the years we have interviewed thousands of successfully married couples and most report a reasonable degree of satisfaction with their sex life. But here is our most important research finding concerning this issue – no marriage was ever saved or made successful because the couple had a great sex life!

And more importantly, when we ask successfully married couples how important sex is to the success of their marriage – to rank on a scale of 1-10 with 10 high – the average rank was 6. This finding has held true over the 26 years of our research. That's hardly a resounding endorsement for the importance of sex in a marriage.

You see, marriage is a multi-faceted relationship, and in the best marriages no one aspect stands out as the make or break part of it. The truth is, and as we report in our book *Golden Anniversaries: The Seven Secrets of Successful Marriage*, there are seven pervasive characteristics present in all successful marriages. And guess what, sex is not one of them!

As we say so often in our many interviews and writings, all of the married couples representing the best marriages we have interviewed have shared with us the importance of touching in their relationship. One gentleman we interviewed told us that if he passed his wife in the house a hundred times a day, he touched her. To touch someone you love is to acknowledge their presence and to communicate your love for them. That's why the most successfully married couples amongst us do it so often.

In our humble opinion, the minister's charge to his congregation to have sex seven days next week not only cheapens the importance of healthy and positive sex with someone you love, but it also reinforces the silliness that great sex will save your marriage – that sex is the centerpiece of all good marriages.

As you know from our many writings, we believe that the overemphasis on sex in books about love and marriage cause people to believe that if they don't have stupendous sex everyday there is something wrong with their marriage. Trust us on this – marriages that fail do so for a variety of reasons and not for a ***single*** reason.

We are sure the good Reverend is well intentioned with his challenge to his congregation, but we believe his advice is misguided as it once again overemphasizes the importance of sex in marriage. To single out sex is to blow its importance entirely out of proportion to its relevance to a great marriage. We wish people would stop doing that!

We reported many first hand accounts from successfully married couples who emphasized how important the human touch is to a loving marriage. They hug each other often, they kiss, they touch each other while talking, they sit cheek to cheek on the couch while having a conversation, they curl around each other when they sleep or just gaze at the stars, and yes, they have sex from time to time – when it's right for them and not forced by some arbitrary "have sex everyday rule!"

You see, people touch each other in many, many different ways and no single form of touching wins the day. It's what we like to call "the accumulation of touching" that matters. Touch the one you love often and in whatever gentle way your heart desires. It's that human connection that wins the day – and wins the marriage! The simple truth is, the best marriages engage in a lot of touching, sex is only one of them.

Touch well! Love well!

CHAPTER 52

Love and Marriage In Retirement

Whether one or both of you worked outside of the home, you are now retired, together in the house alone . . . just you and your spouse . . . now what?

YOU SPENT A LIFETIME TOGETHER raising children, going to work, going to meetings, and in general, meeting everyone else's needs. Whether one or both of you worked outside of the home, you are now retired, together in the house alone . . . just you and your spouse . . . now what?

If you are among the lucky ones, you will get to retire someday and spend more time with your spouse. Actuarially, a retired couple at age 65 has a reasonable chance of spending two more decades of life together until "death do us part." The question is, how do you make these 20 years together enjoyable, fun and exciting?

We are certainly not interested in being morbid about the prospects of death, but as Charley's mother used to say, "You are not going to get out of this world alive!" The truth is, death is a natural part of life. It is inevitable. So, the question becomes, how do you spend those nearly two decades of life with the one you love doing the things you want to do while free of the burdens and stresses associated with work? This question is one all married couples must ultimately deal with if they are lucky.

In a few weeks we are going to be interviewed about love and marriage in retirement so we have been gleaning a lot of information from the many interviews we have conducted over the years with successfully married couples over the age of 65. We think you will find the results interesting.

1. ***Take the time to get to know each other again when one or both of you retire!*** When we first heard this notion years ago we were somewhat taken aback by it. After all, these couples had been married for 30 or more years! Why would they have to get to know each other again? The truth is, the hectic pace of life for so many years – much of it outside the home and family – does change many of the dynamics of the marital relationship. For example, the various responsibilities of running a home, raising children, and the like while one or both work outside the home often change when retirement comes along. And the simple truth is, many of those who retire need to renew many aspects of their loving relationship.

   We have come to believe so strongly in this notion of "renewal" that we included a section in the Appendix of our book, *Golden Anniversaries: The Seven Secrets of Successful Marriage*, entitled "A Seven-Week Program for Developing Ongoing Sharing in Your Marriage." Couples report to us all the time about how much the Seven-Week Program helped them during their retirement transition.

2. ***Never wile away your hours together everyday in front of the television!*** It's a trap so many fall into when they retire. Take a walk, plan a trip, visit your grandchildren, plant a garden, go dancing – plan activities that keep you active and that you can enjoy together. Becoming a couch potato or a back porch rocker is not good for either you or your spouse. Plan something to do outside the home every day. Stay active. Stay healthy. Stay tuned to events in the world surrounding you. Stay young!

3. ***Respect the need for privacy and aloneness in yourself and your spouse.*** You will both be better off for it. The worst thing you can do to your spouse or yourself when one or both of you retire is hover over each other all the time. Just as you need alone time before retirement, you need it after retirement. As you have heard us report in our writings and in *Golden Anniversaries,* there is a fundamental predisposition in every human being to have time alone. Everybody needs time to be with their own thoughts, with their own hobbies, with just themselves. Being retired may give you more time to be together, but couples often forget that the need to be alone is just as strong and just as important when you retire.

4. ***Build a social network of family and friends. Don't become isolated!*** And as much as you would like not to believe this, most of the people you worked with will move on with their lives when you retire. You won't hear from most of them again. They are not being mean or cruel to you. It's just the way life is. You will need to make new friends, meet new acquaintances, build new relationships, and establish new social networks.

5. ***Be spontaneous with much of your day.*** Having unencumbered time is, perhaps, the greatest gift of retirement. Think about it – all those years you worked at a job, raised kids, volunteered – you rarely had unencumbered time. We, like the couples we have interviewed over more than two decades of life, have this insatiable need from time to time to plan nothing for the day! In many ways, those are the best days of our lives together as it is for many of the retired couples we have interviewed. Oh, don't get us wrong. Sometimes you have to plan your day, but not everyday!

6. ***Never take the health of yourself or your spouse for granted.*** The health of a spouse is of profound importance. Successfully married retired couples we have interviewed care deeply about each other's health. Their advice – plan an exercise program together. Eat lots of fruits and vegetables. Take your medicine(s) as prescribed. Keep your weight under control. You see, healthy people live longer. And isn't it comforting to know that you did everything you could to add to those years together and to improve the quality of each other's lives.

7. ***Manage your finances together once retirement occurs.*** The worst thing that can happen according to one of the couples we interviewed is to "outlive your money!" Frankly, life has no guarantees so the best strategy is to manage your resources together, often with the help of a professional financial planner, and with the assumption you will live longer than you might anticipate in an actuarial sense. Our successfully married retired couples have told us repeatedly that they cannot emphasize enough the importance of working together to manage your finances in retirement.

In retirement, the simple things still matter. Love well!

CHAPTER 53

Successful Marriage: Until Death Do Us Part

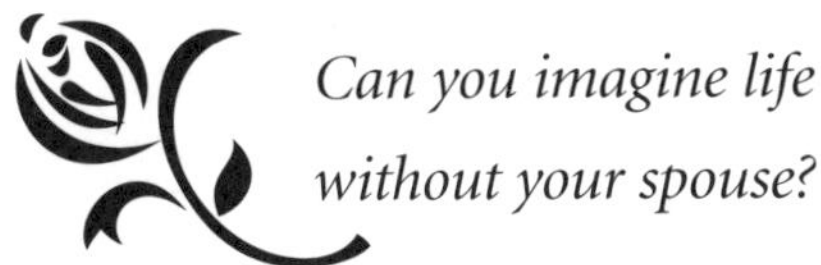

Can you imagine life without your spouse?

AT THE END OF EACH INTERVIEW we conduct with happily and successfully married couples we ask the most powerful question of our interview protocol – "Can you imagine life without your spouse?" The question always draws tears to the eyes of the couple we are interviewing. We have asked them a question they have repressed. It is a question no loving couple wants to think about. The answer is, however, nearly always the same – "No!"

When we take our marriage vows – "until death do us part" – we never imagine that some day it will all come to an end. But all marriages and relationships do end, of that you can be sure. So, how do we prepare for it?

Our advice is, never dwell on or contemplate the question. It doesn't matter. What is important is that we love our spouse, that we enjoy our spouse, and that we live our life with them to the fullest. If you think about the inevitable, your relationship will end in a different way. Yes, a different way.

Here is how it works. If you spend your time imagining the end you will never do all of the things required to deal with the beginning and the middle. You will lose the richness and beauty of each moment. You will, in the end, misplace the essence of your relationship with each other. Your relationship will be based on the end instead of the possibilities.

When you cannot imagine life without the one you love, you have reached the "nirvana" of your loving and committed relationship. But to dwell on the inevitable end of your life together diminishes the here and now and spoils all the joy that lies ahead.

WHY IS LOVE MORE SPECIAL ON HOLIDAYS?

SIMPLE THINGS MATTER

CHAPTER 54

Simple Things Matter During the Holidays

Every family has its own holiday traditions and if your family is lucky they will carry them on year after year after year.

TRUTH IS, WE MISS OUR PARENTS and our grandparents. True to the natural course of life, they are all gone now. They were parents in life and, in many ways, parents in death. They all lived long lives. They all lived full and productive lives. And they all loved the holiday season because of the simple things.

The holiday season is truly a season for all. Nearly all faiths, religions, and ways of life find something to celebrate during this important season. Whatever your faith, whatever your beliefs, always remember this – simple things matter during the holidays.

The most important part of the holiday season has to do with the family traditions we have started along the way and that continue from generation to generation. Many of those traditions have to do with the food we prepare for those special holiday meals. To this day, we make Grandma Uthe's time-honored German potato salad every Christmas.

Our daughter enjoys making baked vegetable kugel with her children every Hanukkah. She started her new family tradition several years ago.

Years ago, Liz started a tradition all her own – making the best turkey stuffing in the entire universe, and beyond! Our whole family can't wait to scarf down generous portions of her delectable dressing. The turkey comes second!

Charley's grandma on his mother's side always put lemon drops wrapped in cellophane on the Christmas tree for the grandchildren. Aunt Vi placed cellophane wrapped chocolate drops on the tree as her annual tradition.

The family holiday tradition in Liz's family was stringing fresh popped popcorn. But the truth is they ate most of the popcorn before it got on the sting! Most popcorn stringing events ended with full tummies, a mess on the kitchen floor, and lots and lots and lots of laughter. Liz still tears up when she teaches the art of popcorn stinging to our two grandchildren.

When Charley was eight years old, his Dad put toy train tracks around the Christmas tree. It left indelible memories in his brain about his Dad and about the tradition he started. Now, when the grandchildren come to town during the holiday season, Charley puts up two trains!

And every Christmas when we decorate the Christmas tree we bake chocolate chip cookies! In fact, we just finished that tradition a few minutes ago!

Memories are made of this, that's for sure. Every family has its own holiday tradition and if your family is lucky they will carry them on year after year after year.

While we recognize that traditions vary from family to family, always remember this – carry them on. Have your own children learn them. Passing them from generation to generation reminds you every special holiday of those you have loved along the way, of those who were kind to you and expressed their love to you through their simple deeds. Traditions as a rule don't usually cost much money, but they last a lifetime.

Over the years, we have written much about the "simple things." And we have always reminded you that simple things matter in love and life. If you do the simple things day in an day out – simple acts of kindness, simple expressions of love, simple homemade gifts and cards, simple traditions – you will enrich not only your life but also the lives of others.

Too often in life, people who love each other make these mistakes:

- You send expensive flowers on an anniversary or holiday but fail to look the one you love in the eyes and tell him or her how much you love them.
- You shower the one you purport to love with expensive gifts instead giving them what they really want – your respect, your understanding, your embrace, your kiss and your time.
- You think that a store bought card is a good substitute for a homemade one!
- You give your children expensive toys when all they want is your love.
- You send grandma and grandpa a card when all they want is for you to call them on the phone.

And the list goes on.

Our final thought for today is this – No love has blossomed or been sustained without doing the simple things. Start today.

CHAPTER 55

Love Is a Timeless New Year's Resolution

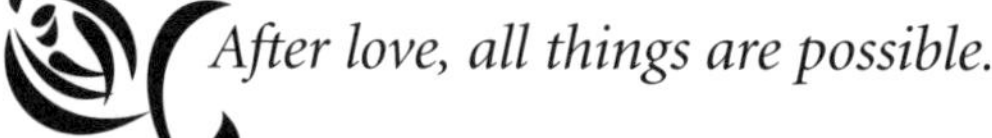

After love, all things are possible.

THIS IS THE TIME OF YEAR when so many of us make promises to ourselves and others that we hardly ever keep! These so-called "New Year's Resolutions" sound good when we make them but, all too often, we ignore them by Valentine's Day.

You know the familiar refrains – I will lose weight. I will quit smoking. I will call my Mom at least once a week! – and the list goes on.

How about you do something different this year. How about making a New Year's Resolution now that you plan to keep. Why not make a commitment to make ***love*** your New Year's Resolution? More importantly, why don't you make a commitment to tell someone you deeply love that you love them – and that you will do it several times every day of the year!

Make this the year that you do not commit the egregious sin of saying, "Oh, I don't need to tell her (him) I love her (him). They know I love them." Wrong! If you love someone you must tell them – you must tell them every day. You must tell them how much you love them and how important they are in your life. You cannot possibly love someone with all your heart and with all your soul and not tell him or her every day. It is simply not possible. Here's why.

We have learned many things from the many lovebirds we have interviewed, but one thing is certain – one thing is pervasive in all of our interviews – people in love say so! They tell each other every day. They shout it to the stars each day. To be in love – to be truly in love – is to tell the one you love that you love them every day of your life. To do less is to diminish your love for them.

Recently, we were in France interviewing successfully married couples. While in Lyon we spent time with the grandparents of one of Charley's exchange students, Barbara, who lives in Lyon with her husband, Francois. Her wonderful grandparents had been in love for nearly 60 years. They reported to us that every day of their lives together they tell each other how much they love each other – how deep their love for each other is. To watch their eyes mist up over the mere mention of their love for each other brought tears to our eyes as well.

We have seen this reaction over and over in the collective ***15,000 years of marriage*** we have interviewed over the past three decades. It's always the same – people in love show their love for each other, but they also TELL their love for each other. They do it every day. To understand why they have stayed married for so long – in this case 58 years – you only have to observe their love for each other and listen to their words. They love each other and they tell each other so many times each day. You can learn a lot from people who are truly in love.

So, friends, when you start making your New Year's Resolutions now, start with love today. After love, all things are possible. Make love your New Year's Resolution for everyday of this year. You will never regret it.

CHAPTER 56

Observing Love on Valentine's Day

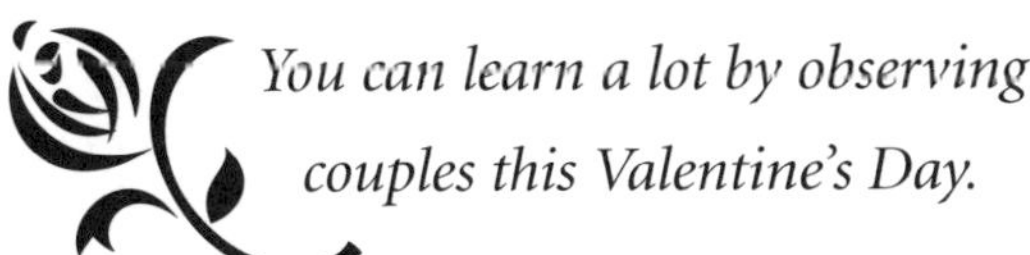

You can learn a lot by observing couples this Valentine's Day.

A COUPLE OF NIGHTS BEFORE Valentine's Day we went out to dinner at a new neighborhood bar and grill. It was snowing outside and very cold so we thought a night out with no cooking responsibilities would be just what the doctor(s) ordered.

We were seated by the host at a window near the restaurant's fireplace. The snow was beautiful as it fell from the sky and the crackling of the fireplace made for a perfect evening. We ordered dinner and a good bottle of wine and engaged in our usual non-stop conversation with each other as we ate and sipped our wine. We called this our ***early*** Valentine's Day dinner because we had a book signing scheduled for several hours on Valentine's Day evening and wouldn't be able to have dinner out.

We have met a lot of people in our quest for knowledge regarding the perfect marriages and relationships, and have interviewed thousands of them. And it's interesting how good our observation skills have become as we have intently observed people in our interviews and in our travels to distant places over the years.

As we continued our meal, our conversation changed to the other couples like us who were out to dinner that night. It dawned on us that we were, in many ways, witnessing what we had written about in our new book. You could actually see love (or the lack thereof) as you observed the couples who were having dinner together. There are lessons to be learned about these couples and we wanted to briefly share them with you. At the end, we will give you a quiz, so pay attention!

Couple 1 sat at the table next to us. The husband was about 50-55 and the wife a little younger, perhaps 45-50. They are married (both had rings on). They were positioned on opposite sides of the dinner table and when they talked to each other (very infrequently), they only moved their heads slightly and rarely made eye contact. Never during the hour did we see them touch. Not once!

Couple 2 was apparently on a date. No rings, and their conversation as they sat down suggested it was a date. She was about 4'11" and he about 6'5". Both were attractive and in their thirties. She looks about as bored with him as one could be unless you enjoy watching paint dry! When the meal was over she leaves the table and waits for him at the door. During dinner they did not touch, rarely talked, and never make eye contact as near as we could tell.

Couple 3 was clearly married. They were both in their 40's. They sit side by side in their dinner booth. Their bodies touch at the legs and shoulders. When they talked they looked directly at each other's face, which was never more than 15 inches apart. She had a look on her face like, "I love every word that comes out of his mouth. He is the most amazing man I have ever met." He looked at her the same way. He obviously is a class clown and is constantly spitting out one-liners that are making her laugh. She was also very touchy with him. They kiss on the lips every now and then. When they leave the restaurant they depart with their arms around each other's waist. She comments to him on the way out that "it was nice to be away from the children for a couple of hours."

Couple 4 are on a date. They were sitting adjacent to us on the right. They were talking when we got to our table and continued to talk the whole time we were there. Their conversation increased in tone and volume over the hour. Her last words, as she stood up, were, "'I'm tired of taking this bulls---t from you. I'm outta here." She walked to the door. He paid the bill and went after her. They disappeared into the night.

We always preach to whoever will listen that in life and love the simple things matter. Do the simple things and your relationship with each other will thrive. To not to do them diminishes the quality of your relationship and is the leading cause of relationship failure. On the other hand, successful love and relationships are an accumulation of the little things.

Now the quiz – if you were to observe these couples having dinner this Valentine's Day, who do you think is the most in love? What couple do you think is living proof of the importance of doing the little things? Which couple, were they all to be married to each other, are most likely to reach their Golden Anniversary together? Couple 3 is, of course, the correct answer. You can learn a lot by observing couples this Valentine's Day. You can learn a lot about love.

CHAPTER 57

A Lifetime of Valentine's Days

Thanks for the memories.
Thanks for your support.
Thanks for being in love.

VALENTINE'S DAY IS ALWAYS a good day to reflect on a lifetime of love. In our case, our love affair with each other has lasted some 42 years. Can you imagine – over four decades of Valentine's Days with one person! And we can tell you this – we have interviewed many couples over the years whose marriage longevity has surpassed ours, dwarfed us – often extending into over six decades of life together.

We remember February 14, 1966 so well. Charley proposed to Liz and then we went dancing until the wee hours of the morning to the sounds of Count Basie. It was so much fun to discover love and to be in love. The Count sealed the deal with his "hold on tight to the one you love" music! What a night! And if you haven't grooved to the sounds of the Count, you should do it today! He was the conductor of the quintessential American jazz orchestra. Getting his autograph that night was wonderful! In fact, we still remember to this day his words after he did so – "Hey, man, can I borrow this pen to sign autographs for other's?" "Of course," Charley said. The Count passed on but the memories of him live on every Valentine's Day.

Ever since Charley proposed to Liz on Valentine's Day in 1966, our lives together have been a continuing celebration of this important anniversary of love. On February 14, 1977 Charley passed the final oral examination over his doctoral dissertation. Dr. Charles D. Schmitz came into being that day. And three years later, Liz passed her final oral examination over her dissertation on Valentine's Day as well, and another Dr. Schmitz was born! Dr. and Dr. Schmitz – "the marriage doctors."

By now, you have figured out that Valentine's Day is an important day in the lives of Charley and Liz. You figured right! It gets better. On Valentine's Day, 1982 we began the research project about successful marriage that led to the publication of our last book entitled, *Golden Anniversaries: The Seven Secrets of Successful Marriage.* And as you have probably guessed, we finished the final product on Valentine's Day, 2007.

So here we are on Valentine's Day and tonight we will do a book signing before and after the romantic concert by Michael Feinstein at the Touhill Performing Arts Center in St. Louis. Some 1400 people are expected. We are excited about sharing the gift of love on Valentine's Day with so many people.

So here we are – full circle. A Valentine's Day filled with celebration, memories, love and hope – filled with friends like you.

Thanks for the memories. Thanks for your support. Thanks for being in love.

CHAPTER 58

Memorial Day and Love Forever

You see, true love does not just last for a lifetime, it lasts forever.

TODAY, WE TOOK OFF ON A journey of remembrance. Memorial Day seemed like a good day to embark on this trip down the memory road of love.

We hopped in our Torch Red Mustang Convertible today and headed west out of St. Louis. We traveled down "winery road" in Missouri. Highway 94 was especially beautiful today. The heavy rains of April and May have brought forth a splendiferous display of green colors. You cannot imagine how beautiful Missouri is in the Spring. Since Charley grew up here it is natural that he would love it, but Liz, the California girl, is another story.

Liz fell in love with Missouri and with Charley some 42 years ago. It was love at first sight, and for the next 42 years this California

Girl, Liz, fell in love with Charley and with Missouri more every day. And for over four decades, we have celebrated the great events in our lives with wines from "winery road" in Missouri.

Today's trip down the memory road of love brought forth an avalanche of thoughts about the meaning of love – particularly about love on such a sacred day as Memorial Day.

Charley's Uncle Verney was a war hero. He fought in World War II, participated in the liberation of Paris, and was wounded at the Battle of the Bulge. Frankly, that fateful day changed Verney's life forever. He took a machine-gun shell through his thigh. Miraculously, someone dragged him to the cellar of an abandoned farm house where he nursed his wound by himself for nearly a week. Before his death, Uncle Verney recounted many times how good he felt the day he was saved by an American Medic.

Verney was saved and upon his return, continued his 50-year love affair with Aunt Viola – Vi as she is called by those who loved her most. We remember so well the day Uncle Verney was buried. There was a 21-gun salute before he was laid to rest in the sacred Missouri ground near "winery road."

Verney loved Vi and Vi loved Verney. And contrary to the recent report in the New York Times, Aunt Vi did not suddenly become "unmarried" because Uncle Verney died. Verney was the love of her life and when he died, Aunt Vi knew she would be married to Verney for the rest of her life. Aunt Vi is now approaching 90 but she is still in love with Verney. She is still his blushing bride.

Today, as we culminated our trip down the memory road of love, we visited the gravesite of Charley's parents. They are buried side by side though their deaths were separated by eight years. Standing over the graves today was emotional to say the least. But knowing that their love will "last forever" made today bearable.

You see, true love does not just last for a lifetime, it lasts forever. To be in love is wonderful. To have your love affair last for a lifetime is magnificent. To know that your love will last forever – through eternity – makes you understand how precious Golden Anniversaries are. Being married to the one you love for a lifetime and beyond is one of the greatest gifts of all.

On this Memorial Day, please remember to cherish those who served their country in the military. And please remember to celebrate your Mom and Dad and your Uncle Verney and Aunt Vi. They will never pass this way again but your memories of them will last for a lifetime and beyond.

Love well. Love forever.

CHAPTER 59

Parents, Love and Holidays

A parent's love is with you everywhere.

A PARENT'S LOVE IS WITH YOU everywhere. Every time you are far from home you are never alone. Your parents are always with you. They think about you. They worry about you. They always love you. They love you no matter what.

Truth is, most parents have unconditional love for their children – no matter the age of the parents or the children.

Charley's Dad, rest his soul, died nearly four years ago when he was 88 years old. He was fond of telling Charley almost to the day that he died that he loved him and that he always worried about him. No matter how old Charley got, he knew his Dad was thinking about him. Worrying about him. Praying that he was safe – free from harm.

You see, there is so much more to parenting than bringing you into this world, feeding you, nurturing you, sheltering you, providing for your needs, educating you, worrying about you, and sacrificing for you. Parents love their children more than life itself and would gladly give theirs to save their child.

The problem so often in life, however, is that so many children do not appreciate their parents until they are gone – until they no longer exist on God's earth. For a child there is so much for which to be thankful. Too often they discover this too late. Which brings us to an important message.

In our thousands of interviews over the years for this book, we have heard so many, many positive stories about successful love and relationships. All too often, however, we hear happily married couples lament about their adult children's lack of understanding when it comes to the importance of coming "home for the holidays" – of being with them at Christmas, Hanukah, Thanksgiving, and on their anniversary. There is a recurring theme and it goes like this – while we love our children we are disappointed in the many excuses they give us as to why they can't be home for the holidays or for important anniversaries.

Frankly, in the early years of our marriage we were guilty of the same transgressions when it came to our parents. However, after a few years we began to see the hurt it caused them when we didn't show up for those important milestones in their lives – those important holidays.

Charley remembers so well those many Thanksgivings watching football games with his Dad. And the Thanksgiving Day in 1989 when Charley's Dad handed him the railroad watch he had worn in his pocket for 47 years – well, it was all Charley could do to hold back the tears. His Dad told Charley by that simple act how much he loved him and how much he cared for him. More importantly,

Charley's Dad told him that day how proud of him he was. Even today when Charley tells that story to his friends and family his eyes well up with tears – tears of love and joy.

Liz remembers her mother, Elizabeth, so well. Her mother inspired her. Her Mother loved her unconditionally. Her mother gave her the blessings so necessary for her to marry Charley. And she died only a few months later. It broke Liz's heart. All the things she wanted to tell her Mother. Now, it was too late. Now she only tells her Mother the things she wanted to say in her prayers at night. We have heard so many tell similar stories.

You see, the sad truth is, everybody passes from this Earth. Everybody dies. Every parent dies. And if we are lucky, we get to spend as much time with them as we can. All too often we do not.

Our message today is this – spend as much time with your parents throughout your life as you possibly can. When they are gone, there are no more holidays with them; no more anniversaries with them, and no more time to tell them you love them.

One of the lines from the chapter There Is No Place Like Home For The Holidays read as follows: "The holiday season reminds us all of what we have come to call 'the caveats of life and love.' Namely, people need love, they need family, they need friends, and they need someone to give their love to. Make no mistake about it – people need people. People need to love and to be loved." We would offer that parents especially need YOUR love – especially during the holidays.

Love Well For the Holidays!

CHAPTER 60

There's No Place Like Home for the Holidays

This holiday season give the most cherished gift of all – give your love unconditionally to family, friends and the one you love.

"Oh, there's no place like home
for the holidays,
'Cause no matter how far away you roam,
When you pine for the sunshine of a friendly gaze,
For the holidays, you can't beat
home, sweet home."

This very popular song's lyricist, Al Stillman, was born in New York and was a writer for Radio City Music Hall for 40 years. He had several other big hits, but this song, originally made popular by the great Perry Como, is perhaps, his most famous.

To our way of thinking, this is the perfect "love song" for the holidays! And here's why.

In life, the people who love you the most are your parents, members of your family, your best friends, and, most importantly, the one you love – a spouse, a lover, a mate – the one you give your love to, unconditionally. Frankly, being in love, sharing your love with another, and having the love of important and significant people in your life, is the most cherished love of all.

It seems that the holiday season – Christmas, Hanukah, Kwanza – whatever your religious beliefs are – is a time of celebration. It is a time to be with family and friends. It is a time to be with the one you love. More importantly, it is a time for reflection on loving and being in love.

Over the years, we have been continuously impressed with the importance of being with family over the holiday season. Every couple in love we have interviewed over the years has pointed out to us how much they cherished time with the ones they love during the holiday season. And they will travel to great lengths to do so!

The holiday season reminds us all of what we have come to call "the caveats of life and love." Namely, people need love, they need family, they need friends, and they need someone to give their love to. Make no mistake about it – people need people. People need to love and to be loved.

To state a refrain – there is no place like home for the holidays. Who says you can't go home again? Certainly not someone in love! And if you come home to your family and friends with a new friend or a new lover for them to meet you have added in a geometric way more love to your family, your friends, and yourself.

The truly wonderful thing about going home for the holidays is this – you are reminded over and over again how much you are loved and how much love you have to give. While you bask in the love from family, friends and your loved one this holiday season, remember that your capacity to give love is unlimited. This holiday season give the most cherished gift of all – give your love unconditionally to family, friends and the one you love.

"Oh, there's no place like home for the holidays. 'Cause no matter how far away you roam, when you pine for the sunshine of a friendly gaze, for the holidays, you can't beat home, sweet home."

Cherish your family, your friends, and your lover. There is no greater love. Enjoy the gift of love and of being loved.

Love Well and Happy Holidays!

REFLECTIONS ON MARRIAGE

SIMPLE THINGS MATTER

CHAPTER 61

Traditional Marriage Is Alive and Well

Marriage is alive and well in the USA
and around the world.
To suggest otherwise is to
ignore the real facts.

WE KNOW, WE HEAR THEM all the time – those purveyors of half-truths, un-truths, and political agendas. You know the ones – the ones who continually pronounce to the world that traditional marriage is dead. Well, all we can say is – don't believe it!

Statistically there is substantial support for our point of view. According to the best estimates we can find, there were some 43,500,000 marriages worldwide in 2007. There were 8,750,000 divorces in the same year. If you do the math you can see that worldwide, marriages outnumber divorces by a ratio of 5 to 1. Stated clearly and succinctly, there were five marriages for every one divorce in the world last year. Hardly sounds like the death of marriage to us.

The truth is – based on the facts – marriage is alive and well in the world today. There is no disputing these facts. So, why do the purveyors of negativism continue to distort the truth? Why do certain members of the media and so many of those who write books about the demise of marriage continue to distort the reality of what is?

There are probably lots of reasons to explain this phenomenon. Foremost among them are the polltakers. Polltakers are notorious for asking the wrong questions or asking poorly phrased questions, and then reporting results that are, well, grossly out of touch with the reality they purport to represent.

Here is a recent example. A Zogby Poll got much national attention a short while ago. One of their so-called "findings" was the following: "Issues related to trust in relationships vary significantly among different generations. Younger respondents are more likely to want the truth from their partner, even if it hurts - more than 85% of respondents in their 20s said they always want the truth, compared to 79% of those in their 50s and 60s."

We wonder, did it ever occur to the pollsters that there is a "maturity factor" at work here? Did they ever consider that younger respondents "want the truth" from their partner "even if it hurts" is simply the admonitions of naïve young people who don't yet understand that "sometimes the truth hurts." Older folks have gained great wisdom over the years and they know that sometimes "words hurt." Words sometimes have unintended consequences. Older and wiser people understand this. Older folks tend to be more careful with what they express, especially if their words might have negative consequences.

And one more point about this poll – did anyone ask if the difference between 85% (the percentage of young people who want the truth) and 79% of older adults who always "want the truth" was statistically significant? In every poll, there is an error of measurement. True differences occur outside of this error range. In other words, is the 6% difference reported by the pollster really meaningful?

We offer the aforementioned example to demonstrate that the questions asked and to whom, often determines the answer received. But, the answer received is not always the answer that is the most honest portrayal of the truth or the reality of it all.

Here is another example. A recent *New York Times* article reported that fewer than half of American women were now married. Yet, they included in their population of "un-married women" girls who were 15, 16, and 17 years old and women whose husbands were deceased! See our point? Does anyone really believe that 15-year-old girls are "women?" Of course not! Does anyone really believe that a 70-year-old widow is "unmarried?" Of course not!

So, here is where we are. Marriage is alive and well in the world today! It is still among the greatest structures for social order that exists in the world today. Marriage is not in danger just because a pollster asks a question that suggests it is. Marriage is not in danger just because people who report statistical data report it incorrectly or in a way that leads to a false conclusion about marriage.

The truth is, marriage is alive and well worldwide AND in the United States of America. Marriage is still the greatest and most profound commitment to love that exists, irrespective of the so-called truths exposed by pollsters who might suggest something otherwise based on faulty or distorted polling data.

When you discount for the number of divorcees in America who get divorced multiple times, the "divorce rate" and its impact is much less than that reported by the popular media. As we have said before, the "real" divorce rate in the USA in terms of its true societal impact is far less than the 50% rate reported. When discounted for those who have multiple divorces, the "true" impact divorce rate is probably closer to 35% or 40%.

As researchers for over 26 years, all we ask is that the good folks who read polls and crunch numbers do so very carefully. The conclusions you draw will often be different from those concluded by the pollsters, the popular media, and the so-called experts.

Marriage is alive and well in the USA and around the world. To suggest otherwise is to ignore the real facts.

CHAPTER 62

The Benefits of Marriage

You have many powerful reasons
to work hard to celebrate your
Golden Anniversary with your spouse.

NOW YOU KNOW THAT THE RECIPE for a successful marriage takes a lot of hard work doing the simple things each day, this chapter should convince you that it is absolutely worth whatever it takes for you to achieve a long-term successful marriage. After a lengthy review of the current research on the benefits of marriage, we have selected what we think are the top 10 reasons why you should work hard to achieve a happy successful marriage. It has been proven time and time again that your life can be improved in a great number of ways by staying in a successful long-term marriage!

Top 10 Benefits of Marriage:

Reason #1: You will live longer. The preponderance of evidence from research shows a relationship between longer life and being married. In fact, one study found that married men live an average of ten years longer and married women live an average of four years longer than those who are unmarried.

Reason #2: You will be healthier. There have been a great number of research studies throughout the world since 1987 demonstrating a positive relationship between being married and better physical health. The links between marriage and good physical health are overwhelming. Married individuals have lower rates of serious illness and are less likely to die in hospitals.

Reason #3: You will be happier. Married people report being happier than unmarried people. They are hopeful, happy and feel good about themselves. A multitude of studies demonstrate the same results. In fact, in a 10-year survey involving 14,000 adults, James Davis found that 40% of married individuals were happy with their life compared to only 15-20% of any of the unmarried groups.

Reason #4: You will experience higher levels of psychological health. Married people have lower rates of depression and schizophrenia than unmarried people. They are better balanced and less likely to experience mental illness.

Reason #5: You will have a built-in support system. Research indicates that individuals in a marriage feel supported, saying that they have someone to share their feelings and thoughts with. They always have someone they trust to confide in and to lean on in times of need.

Reason #6: You will be less likely to abuse drugs or alcohol. Numerous studies indicate that married individuals are less likely than unmarried persons to engage in risky behaviors including the use of drugs or alcohol because of their feelings of responsibility.

Reason #7: Your earnings will be greater. Numerous studies found that married men's earnings are significantly greater than unmarried men's earning. The most recent studies of women's earning power demonstrate that married women earn more than unmarried women even when their husband's income is not considered part of their earnings. The vast majority of the studies take all of the various possible factors into consideration and the results still demonstrate greater earnings for married individuals than for unmarried ones.

Reason #8: You will save more money. With enduring marriages couples tend to be more financially responsible. In the United States married individuals in their 50s and 60s have a net worth per person roughly twice that of other unmarried individuals.

Reason #9: You will have sex more often and enjoy it more. Physically and emotionally married couples report a greater satisfaction with sex then their unmarried counterparts. Married couples also have sexual intimacy more often than unmarried couples.

Reason #10: Your children will be healthier, do better academically and have less emotional problems. Children living in families with married parents are more likely to have proper health care, better nutrition and less stress to deal with at home. These children have less serious illnesses and grew up healthier than children not raised in households with married parents.

On average, children who are raised in households with stable marriages enjoy better developmental outcomes than children raised in households with unmarried individuals. These children have significantly better grades, test scores and overall success in school than their counterparts raised in households with unmarried individuals.

The research indicates that children living with married parents have less reported behavioral problems at school or at home than children who do not. They experience better psychological health than children raised in households with unmarried parents or guardians. Your children are less likely to engage in risky behaviors if you remain in a stable marriage. For example, sexual activity, drug, alcohol and weapons use are less likely to occur with children raised in married households. Children have a better opportunity to grow to fully functional adults if married parents raise them.

Linda Gallagher and Maggie Waite, after analyzing the results of their comprehensive study on the benefits of marriage in 1990, suggested that there should be a similar warning about not being married as the Surgeon General's warning on cigarette packages. They want divorce decrees to carry the warning label, "Not being married can be hazardous to your health." They could not have said it better.

When you consider what social science research tells us about the benefits of being married and what our research reveals about the importance of the seven characteristics of successful marriages, you have many powerful reasons to work hard to celebrate your ***Golden Anniversary*** with your spouse.

CHAPTER 63

The Purpose of Marriage – Is It To Have Children?

Marriages thrive and survive more than anything else because of the quality of the relationship between mom and dad.

RECENTLY A GREAT DEAL HAS been reported about the purpose of marriage, lamenting the fact that Americans no longer consider children among the most important purposes of marriage. While most experts are concluding that this is a negative change, we would like to offer a different perspective based on our two and one-half decades of research on successful marriage.

Our principle conclusion is that marriage is alive and well in the United States today. In fact, we have found seven pervasive characteristics present in all successful marriages. And guess what - ***the quality of the relationship between husband and wife trumps everything else in a marriage!*** And you know why - it's simple, really - without a positive, loving, and thriving relationship between mom and dad, children often don't prosper, they are not well-adjusted, they don't do well in school, and they are not as healthy, both physically and mentally.

In all of our interviews over the years with these couples who have a long and successful marriage, not one of them ever mentioned that the purpose of their marriage was to have children. Oh, to be sure, they loved their children very much. They were delighted they brought children into this world and were very proud of them for the most part. But they also reported to us time and time again that it was the strength of their relationship with each other that made their marriage happy and allowed them to attend to all the myriad of responsibilities and issues present in their marriage.

Marriages thrive and survive more than anything else because of the quality of the relationship between mom and dad. It's no more complicated than that.

Let's look at the facts - 73% of women 30 years old and older are currently married or widowed. Most importantly, 94% of all women will have been married at least once by the age of 50.

The truth is, American's love marriage! We just need to learn how to get it right the first time around instead of having nearly four out of every ten of our marriages end in divorce. And the simple truth is, 60% of those that re-marry after divorce get divorced again. So you see, the relationship between mom and dad does trump everything else. Get it right and good things follow. Get it wrong and lots of bad things often happen!

A women quoted in the *Washington Post* got it right when she said, "When I think of marriage I don't think of children at all. I have them. But with marriage, I think of a husband and a wife, and I don't think it's the children that make it work."

The purpose of marriage within the historical and social context is strengthened when the focus is on the development of a strong, positive, and blissful relationship between husband and wife. That relationship trumps everything else. Make this relationship work and everything else follows.

CHAPTER 64

Why Beautiful Women Do NOT Marry Ugly Men

Love trumps everything.
All things are beautiful
in true and lasting love.

WE THINK THE WHOLE "visual thing" when it comes to love and relationships is dramatically overrated. Our research would call into question the study that came out recently entitled "Why Beautiful Women Marry Less Attractive Men." To put it bluntly, the authors of this study are just plain wrong! Their conclusions are flawed. Here's why.

Women do NOT marry less attractive men! They marry men they have fallen in love with. We tend to marry people we judge to be most like us -- socio-economically like us, people we think are in our "beauty class," people who agree with us on most issues, people who share our core values, etc. Our perception of the way another person looks does affect whether or not we are attracted to them in the beginning, but then a whole new set of dynamics takes over. Once attracted, for whatever reason, love takes over. That's why you see couples that look like Mutt and Jeff – couples who are fat and skinny, tall and short, and so forth. Love, pardon the pun, does from time to time make for strange bedfellows!

Interestingly enough, people who have had a long and successful loving relationship have reported to us that they think the one they love is beautiful no matter what other's assessment of their relative looks might be. Successfully married couples, for example, report to us that they simply love their partner and in the list of things that matter in their relationship, the physical part, beyond being healthy, matters very little. Love is love no matter its shape or size or its relative beauty. Your love is your love no matter what others may think about it or how they might assess it. Being in love with another person does not require approval or acceptance by others. Love is personal and the reasons for it are often known only to the people in love. But in the end, that is probably all that matters.

Beauty is relative and resides in the eyes of the beholder. When you fall in love, you will do so based on your own perceptions of the other person and the value you place on what you see. Others are not capable of telling you what matters to you in that relationship. In the end, the goodness of your partner, their honesty and trustworthiness, and the core values you share, will win out. Love trumps everything. All things are beautiful in true and lasting love.

CHAPTER 65

Love, Marriage and Pre-Nuptial Agreements

Frankly, we don't believe that the true meaning of "marriage" allows for this sort of duplicitous relationship between two people who say they love each other.

WE BELIEVE THAT PRE-NUPITIAL agreements are a bad idea, period! Just imagine, telling someone that you love him or her, but you don't trust them! To us, this is analogous to having two separate checking accounts in a marriage -- one for him and one for her. In both cases it becomes a case of yours and mine. Or, how about this, "I love you with the following conditions." Whatever happened to US? We? Love without conditions?

Frankly, we don't believe that the true meaning of "marriage" allows for this sort of duplicitous relationship between two people who say they love each other. True love means true love. You can't have a bonafide loving and successful marriage or relationship when you have a Pre-Nuptial Agreement! People who invented this concept don't know anything about real love and real relationships. Only people with an agenda would encourage something so anti-love, so anti-relationship, and so anti-marriage.

The sad news -- in the United States, prenuptial agreements are recognized in all fifty states and the District of Columbia. Why do we need them? What ever happened to pure, unconditional love! We believe it still exists! It is still the norm, thank goodness!

According to Wikipedia, "There are two types of prenuptial agreements: a *marriage contract* for people who are married or about to be married, and a *cohabitation agreement* for unmarried couples. A variation for people who are already married is a *post-nuptial agreement.*" We think all three are bad for love, bad for relationships, and bad for marriage. Here's why.

In our research with successfully married couples over the years, we have found a number of recurring and pervasive themes. Foremost among them is an abiding trust in and for each other. They trust each other completely and without conditions. People who truly love each other do so without conditions. They have unconditional love – as it should be.

Some would argue that since 35% to 40% of all marriages end in divorce and nearly two-thirds of the marriages of re-married folks face a similar fate, signing a pre-nuptial agreement is only prudent and sensible. It is insurance against a failed relationship.

To us, this is like saying, "Let's never get married because our chances of failure are great." Or, "Let's not fall in love at all because we might fall out of love in the future." Pretty silly, huh?

Like most things in successful relationships, the simple things matter. Caring deeply for someone – loving someone – is only as real as the honesty of the relationship between the two people who profess to love and care for each other.

We ask you these questions:

- ***Do you truly and deeply love someone else?***
- ***Do you care for another human being more that you care for yourself?***
- ***Is there someone in your life that you would die for?***
- ***Is there someone you would like to spend the rest of your life on Earth with?***
- ***Is there someone you share your deepest and darkest secrets with?***
- ***Is there someone that you cannot imagine life without?***

If the answers to all of the questions above are yes, you are completely and wonderfully in love. People like you do not need a pre-nuptial agreement. What you do need to do is spend your lives together. What you do need to do is cement your relationship with each other. What you do need to do is all of the simple things required to make your marriage or relationship work. What you don't need to do is sign a pre-nuptial agreement!

CHAPTER 66

Love and Marriage In France

The greatest romantic country in the world –
and a very secular country as well –
is getting interested in marriage again.

RECENTLY, WE AGAIN TRAVELED to Europe to conduct more interviews with successfully married couples for our next book entitled, *Love and Marriage in Romantic Countries.* Since we had not been to France in several of years, we were beginning to believe the media reports about how the French did not like Americans. So, we braced ourselves for the difficulties we might encounter as two American authors and researchers asking intimate questions about love and marriage in France. Our fears and the media reports could not have been further from the truth.

First of all, the French people were delightful! They were wonderfully warm, open, friendly and courteous beyond imagination.

Everywhere we went they treated us like members of their family. From the hotels we stayed in to the local bistros, the people were marvelous. On buses, trains, subways, and in cabs, we were greeted with open arms and great warmth.

And while we have heard for years the notion that "French people will be more friendly if you speak to them in French," we found that a warm handshake and a big smile spoke volumes in French! They were polite to us and we reciprocated. We struggled with each other's languages but we managed. Big smiles, hand signs, and hugs go a long way in most of the foreign countries we have visited. That's for sure.

Our travels took us throughout France, with a focus on Paris and Lyon—both wonderful cities with fabulous cuisine, great wine, sights to behold, and history to tell. But more than anything, with all the amenities of these two great cities, we were struck by the friendliness and warmth of the French people. We were there for nearly two weeks and only have splendid experiences to report. The French passion for food, wine, life and romance cannot be missed if you just strike up a conversation with someone, observe couples strolling down the Champs Elysee, or when you mingle in a small café or bistro.

And the couples we interviewed were marvelous, which brings us to the main point of our story. You have probably heard that the French are no longer interested in marriage or some variation on that theme. Don't you believe it! The couples we interviewed who had been successfully and happily married for 30 to 77 years reported great satisfaction in their marriage and would do it all over again. But here is where it gets interesting – we found the same themes in young French couples that were in love. The ones we interviewed loved each other very much and were looking forward to getting married, just like their aunts and uncles, parents, and grand parents before them. In fact, the word on the French streets is that marriage is making a very nice comeback in France! We heard nothing while we were there to dispute that notion.

Isn't that wonderful news! The greatest romantic country in the world – and a very secular country as well – is getting interested in marriage again. That is encouraging news, indeed.

When we summarized our recent interview data from France we were struck by how similar the characteristics that defined their successful marriages and relationships were to those in the USA. They were virtually identical. It seems that successful marriages around the world or in romantic countries have common themes. Frankly, we continue to be extremely excited about our findings.

Prior to this visit some of the countries where we had already interviewed couples over the years are Argentina, Australia, Austria, Belgium, Brazil, Canada, Chile, China, Denmark, France, Germany, Great Britain, Greece, Italy, Luxembourg, Mexico, Monaco, Norway, Portugal, Spain, Sweden, Switzerland, Taiwan, The Philippines and The Netherlands. On our most recent trip we interviewed additional couples in Belgium, Great Britain, France, and Luxembourg. Next we are off to South Africa to interview couples with successful marriages of more than 30 years.

While we have enjoyed immensely the couples we have interviewed in all of the countries we have visited, we particularly enjoyed our recent interviews with French couples. There are a multitude of reasons why. But if you pushed us to name just one, it would have to be their passion for enjoying the romance of life and their love for each other. We do not ever remember feeling so comfortable and welcomed by the people of a foreign country than we did in our recent trip to France.

As we began to write the individual and collective stories of these engaging French couples with successful marriages for our next book, we found ourselves wanting to share some of those findings with you now. We were just too excited to wait!

CHAPTER 67

Reflections on Love and Marriage

Being in love and being loved is a great way to spend your life.

WE JUST CELEBRATED OUR 42nd Wedding Anniversary. Just imagine, being successfully married for 42 years! And as a friend of ours used to say, "And to the same person!" Having a successful marriage is certainly a worthy life goal. We are well on our way to being one of those fortunate couples who celebrate their golden anniversaries.

While we spend a lot of time studying and writing about the successful long-term relationships of others, we decided to spend some time today thinking about our own wonderful marriage that has spanned more than four decades of our lives.

One of our favorite lines from a song says it all – "Still crazy after all these years." That's the way we feel about each other – still crazy in love after all these years.

Forty-three years ago, a small town Missouri boy met a California girl at College. His friends were the sons and daughters of Missouri farmers and other good folks who worked on the railroad. Her friends were California surfers and swimmers. She was bronze colored, tall, and had that look of a long-distance swimmer. It was fun for Charley to see her walking down the sidewalk, grooving to the sounds of the Beach Boys as her hair blew in the wind. He still marvels today at how much he loved her then and how much more he loves her today. Think golden anniversaries!

Liz used to listen for hours while Charley sang Elvis songs to her. She once said, "Gosh, you really do sound like him!" Charley turned red, but he was proud. Elvis was his hero. And now Liz was!

Liz tells Charley every day how much she loves him and how she couldn't imagine life without him. Charley smiles, then cries. It feels so good to be loved so much. He reflects on his life with Liz and wonders how he got so lucky. He loves to tell everyone within earshot how he "married up!" He swears that most men do. Liz says she feels the same way about him. Hmmmm . . . maybe we both married up!

It's always fun for us to reflect on life together. We have so, so many common interests. We are alike in many, many ways. But through it all we have maintained our individuality and our respective identities – with enormous respect for our differences as well as our similarities.

By the measures we articulated in the chapter called *How Will I Know I Am In Love?* it is still clear that we are still crazy in love after all these years.

Helping others build loving relationships that last a lifetime has become one of our greatest goals in life. Being in love and being loved is a great way to spend your life. And while we truly and sincerely believe that successful loving relationships are not all that difficult to understand and make work, we continue to be surprised by the fact that so many "people in love" won't do the simple things required to make their love last.

On the occasion of our 42nd Wedding Anniversary we renewed our commitment to help others learn the important lessons about love and relationships so that they can practice the simple truths about love everyday of their lives together.

May your love be as strong as ours and your commitment to make your love work even stronger. Go be happy and in love. There is nothing like it. Let's celebrate our Golden Anniversaries together!

EPILOG

SIMPLE THINGS MATTER

EPILOG

Is My Marriage Worth Saving?

The simple truth is, some marriages and relationships should not and cannot be saved.

WE HAVE SAID FOR MANY years, "Most marriages and relationships can be saved, but not all!" And our corollary has always been – "Most marriages and relationships are worth saving, but not all!" Here's what we mean.

In the case of abuse – sexual, physical, mental – many failing marriages and relationships are simply not worth saving. In fact, to attempt to save them puts one or both partners in the relationship at risk for further abuse.

Frankly, we know that some marriages and relationships are not worth saving. And do you know how hard this statement is to make for people like us – the eternal optimists who always see a pot of gold at the end of the rainbow—who always see a silver lining? Unfortunately, the truth is the truth when it comes to love and life . . . and marriage.

Our six decades of life and nearly three decades of research on the topics of love and marriage, tell us that some relationships become so poisoned, so dysfunctional, and so hopeless, that it is better to end them than to operate under the illusion that they are worth saving or can be saved.

We recently interviewed a young American couple that had been married for 14 years. It was clear from the beginning of the interview that this was not a match made in heaven. In fact, this marriage had failed so miserably that the only just and decent thing to do was end it. End it now! No amount of counseling and therapy, no amount of praying, and no amount of hoping were going to save this marriage.

For 14 years, the husband had "mentally abused" his wife. He discounted her every word. He made her feel insignificant by his words, his deeds, and by his actions. And even though his wife was pursuing a doctoral degree at one of America's most prestigious universities, he treated her like she was some kind of dumb cluck – someone capable of nothing significant, lasting, or meaningful.

When we interviewed them, it became clear to us that she had had enough. She had had enough of his disrespect, his belittling, his mental abuse, and his coldness. She had finally decided that if she were to have any life at all, their marriage and their relationship would have to become history. So, she decided to end it.

The truth is, the mental anguish she suffered over the years had taken its toll – on her, her three children, and on her marital relationship. She asked us the most profound question of all – "How can I continue to live with a man that makes me feel so worthless, so insignificant, and so meaningless. How can I continue to live with a man that respects me so little?"

Her questions reveal the truth of all this. Sometimes it is just time to move on. Sometimes, to save your soul you have to free yourself of all that is oppressive. Sometimes, you must remove the albatross around your neck if you have any hope of living out your life with happiness, hope, self-respect, and meaningfulness.

Sometimes, you simply must move on with your life before it is too late. For the couple we interviewed, her time had come. The action she must take was clear. The action she must take to save her soul and the souls of her three children became clear to her – if she had any hope at all for her life and her children's lives, the time to move on was now!

The simple truth is, some marriages and relationships should not and cannot be saved. As harsh and evident as this truth is, it cannot be avoided in the case of some marriages and relationships. And in the end, when you have exhausted the solutions available to you, you simply must cut the tithes that bind.

For more than 26 years now, we have interviewed couples around the world and across cultures and continents. Most of the time we have concluded that most marriages and relationships can and should be saved – but not all! When you can look in the mirror and honestly and truthfully say that you did your best to save your relationship with another human being, but to no avail, then ending it is the right thing to do. Life is too short to waste it in torment, in abuse, and in lost love.

Save yourself.

Special Thanks

WHEN YOU ENGAGE IN A "labor of love" for more than 26 years, there are a lot of people to thank, especially when your work culminates in a finished book like *Simple Things Matter in Love and Marriage.* We have worked with many wonderful people along the way, but several stand out.

First and foremost, we would like to thank all of those marvelous and wonderful couples we have interviewed over the years. We have learned so much from them about love, successful marriage, and relationships. They were and continue to be an inspiration for us, and a model for successful marriage in the USA and around the world.

When it comes to graphic designers, there is no one better than Sandy Morris. We simply love the cover she created for this book. She is the best! Sandy has been our "graphic designer of choice" for nearly twelve years. More importantly, we are blessed by her friendship and support.

Our colleague, David Riklan, at www.selfgrowth.com, provided us the opportunity to greatly expand our work via the Internet. His offer for us to become the Official Guides to Marriage on SelfGrowth.com has changed our lives. It gave us unbelievable "platform" for our work. Our writings about love and marriage are now read around the world. Thank you, David. You have changed our lives!

We are especially indebted to our "editor of choice," Pat Kloepfer. PK, as she is called by her friends, has a great eye for detail. Her eagle eye catches our mistakes. She has been a loyal friend and editor for over a decade. Thanks, PK!

We are especially proud of the accomplishments of our daughter, Kristina, and for blessing us with two wonderful grandchildren, Hudson and Hope. When her children came into our lives we understood once and for all the meaning of "eternity." You live on through your children and grandchildren. Life is good.

In addition, we owe a huge debt of gratitude to the wonderful folks at both Walsworth and Briarcliff Publishing companies. They have stood beside us over the years and took us on when others doubted the importance of our work. All we ever wanted to do with our books is promote the positive benefits of successful marriage. They believed in our "successful marriage projects" and we will be forever indebted to them for their support.

And to our friends at the Gallup Organization, Don Clifton (rest his soul), Cheryl Beamer, Gary Gordon, Jim Clifton, and Tim Simon, we want to thank you for teaching us to understand that if you want to know something about success, study success. We have followed your advice over the years and thank you for your support from the bottom of our collective hearts.

Finally, we have been lovebirds for some 43 years. We believe in each other and in ourselves. Our marriage has been blessed with a beautiful daughter, two amazing grandchildren, and a marital relationship that has transcended time. Nearly 43 years of successful marriage is a testament to our enduring love for each other.

Love well!

Our Wonder Dog Jake

And yes, the heart on his forehead is real.

SIMPLE THINGS MATTER

My Reflections on Love and Marriage